How to Lead Your Child to Christ

Tyndale House Publishers, Inc., Wheaton, Illinois

How to
Lead Your
Child
to Christ

ROBERT & BOBBIE
WOLGEMUTH

To Danae Ann Dobson and James Ryan Dobson

CD Playlist

Into My Heart
Holy! Holy! Holy!
What Can Wash Away My Sin?
I Have Decided to Follow Jesus
Trust and Obey
The Apostles' Creed
The Lord's Prayer

SPECIAL THANKS TO:

Mr. Larry Hall, producer/arranger
Mr. Kent Madison, recording engineer
Mr. John Duncan, executive producer of the musical recording for
Hymns for a Kid's Heart, volumes 1 and 2, Crossway Books
Mrs. Lynn Hodges, children's choir director
Miss Abby Schrader, soloist and reader
Miss Alex Taylor, soloist

*We are deeply grateful for the contributions of each of these friends
and accomplished professionals.*

Table of Contents

Welcome!

"I have no greater joy than to hear that my children walk in the truth" (3 John 1:4).

This Bible verse stood as a sentry, keeping watch over Samuel and Grace Wolgemuth's family. It guarded them the moment they gently took their first child—Ruth Ann—in their arms on a bitter cold January morning in 1941.

Two and a half years later, in July of 1943, a second baby—a son named Samuel—was born. A few weeks later, while standing in the narthex of the tiny Pennsylvania church that her husband pastored, Grace watched as a man approached her. He glanced down at the newborn, wrapped tightly in a blanket and sleeping soundly in her arms.

"What guarantee do you have that this child will know God?" he asked stiffly, making no effort at tenderness or diplomacy. Mother stood in stunned silence for just a moment, wondering at his rudeness; then the promise of the Lord to Isaiah washed over her: "I will contend with him who contends with you, and I will save your children" (Isaiah 49:25).

My mother knew that parents cannot guarantee the salvation of their children, since that is their own to claim. She also knew that the biblical text from Isaiah wasn't written for mothers holding their newborn children in church foyers, but she believed that God was sovereign and could comfort her with this promise at just the right time. And so He did.

Now God's sentry who stood guard over my parents' family had a battle cry: "I will save your children."

Samuel Wolgemuth died in the winter of 2002. But sixty-four years—five children, twenty grandchildren, and eighteen great-grandchildren—after Ruth Ann was born, my mother relentlessly holds on to these promises today.

Following Samuel and Grace's example, the same confidence in God's saving grace has been claimed on our daughters and their families. We have experienced no greater joy than to see our children—and their kids—walk in God's truth. And because of our own sinfulness, this treasure has not been secured because of our deftness or cleverness . . . but by God's faithfulness and grace. All along we have had the assurance that the battle for their soul was in the hands of the Mighty One—the Lord God of Abraham, Isaac, and Jacob.

❊ ❊ ❊

One of the things we talked about with our longtime friends Jim and Shirley Dobson in 1981, over what would be the first of many dinners together, was their claim of these same truths for their own kids.

"Our single most important priority," Shirley told us, "is that our children know Jesus Christ, love Him, and follow Him." Jim was in complete agreement.

We were introduced to the influence that Jim's mother and dad had on him as a young boy and their persistent prayers for his salvation. And in that moment of shared dreams, the four of us became close friends, recommitting to a lifetime of prayer for our own—and now for each other's—children. So when the idea for the book was presented to us, we immediately knew that this decades-old pledge would be the book's centerpiece—thus the dedication to their children, Danae Ann and James Ryan.

In this little book, we would love to draw you into our circle. Pull up a chair, there's plenty of room.

The goal is to provide you with a guidebook that will help you teach your children what it means to know Jesus Christ as their personal Savior. We will explain how to take your children's hands and encourage them to embark on their own friendship with the living God.

Most of this book is for you as the parent to read and understand. Some of the material may be familiar. Some of it may be brand-new. We hope that what you already know will be confirmed and the new information will be helpful. It's important for you to understand more than your children can comprehend at their young age. And it's important for you to grow in your own knowledge of God's Word and in your relationship with Christ so that you'll be able to clearly speak of God's truth to your family.

Each chapter also includes one or more sidebars with some practical ideas on how you can encourage your children to grow in their faith. At the end of each chapter, there is a story—clearly marked—for you to read to them. These stories will take an idea from the chapter and put it into a format your kids can follow. The enclosed CD, which includes five familiar hymns brimming with great doctrine, is to share with your kids as well. With the CD playing in your car stereo during just a few trips to the store or to school, your children will have this Bible truth memorized.

> *A child's receiving the gift of God's grace is* truth, *settled in a* moment, *confirmed through* daily experience, *and stretched out over a* lifetime.

The delightful fact is that in a Christian home, the experience of salvation is also a process. A child's receiving the gift of God's grace is *truth*, settled in a *moment*, confirmed through *daily experience*, and stretched out over a *lifetime*. Often parents are both the obstetrician, introducing their kids to a new birth of faith, and the pediatrician, nurturing the new spiritual life in their children. Our prayer is that this is exactly what happens to you.

Thank you for joining us in this marvelous adventure. Welcome and God bless you . . . and your family.

ROBERT & BOBBIE WOLGEMUTH
Orlando, Florida

INTRODUCTION
One Girl's Story

A True Story to Read to Your Children

My name is Mrs. Wolgemuth. You can call me Miss Bobbie, as the kids in our neighborhood call me. I am a grandmother with grandchildren like you, and I know a little girl who has asked me to tell you her story but would like to keep her name a secret. You can be sure that every bit of her story is true, because she wanted you to know just what happened to her when she was only eight years old.

Let me start by telling you that this little girl had everything most children would ever dream of owning. Her father was a doctor and often brought home wonderful gifts and toys for his daughter. And her mother was a beautiful woman who wore fancy clothes and lovely jewelry. This girl lived in a big, red brick house and went swimming, played tennis, or rode her bike whenever she liked. A very proper English nanny took care of the girl and her sisters during the week while their mother was out attending tea parties, fashion shows, and other special events. On Sundays, everyone in the family slept late except her dad, who played golf at the country club nearby.

Most people would say the hazel-eyed youngster was a nice enough girl, with a lot of talent. She took piano lessons and enjoyed playing for her mother's friends. And, even though she had what most people would call a very nice life, this little girl told me that she often felt sad and angry on the inside. Sometimes she thought about doing mean things when no one was watching, like the day at school when she decided to use really wicked words, yelling some mean things to a classmate when the teacher wasn't listening. Yes, this girl told me that she acted sweet and kind in front of grown-ups, but on the inside she had hateful, ugly feelings and was very selfish.

One of the best things this girl remembers about her life as a kid is that a family of angels lived across the street from her house. I say angels because that is what the girl herself called them. Their real names were Mr. and Mrs. Lay—Homer and Libby. They had a daughter named Martha, and the neighbor girl from our story says she was the brightest angel of all. Why, even when faced with this spoiled little neighbor, Martha would be kind and play with her. Even though Martha did not have as many toys or fancy clothes as her neighbor, there *was* something Martha had that made the little girl want to go to Martha's house whenever she could. Do you want to know what it was?

Well, there was so much love at Martha's home that it spilled onto everyone who walked in the door. Her mother usually greeted the neighborhood kids with a smile, a hug, and a "Welcome children; please come inside." Then Mrs. Lay would sit and talk and ask questions about the children's day. Sometimes she would let them hold the new baby named Ann. Near the end of most visits, everyone would go over to the brown piano in the corner of the playroom and sing some special songs.

The girl who told me the story said that at night when she was alone in bed she would think about that family across the street. Why did she feel so special there? She wondered what made Martha's family so different from her own. She thought about the words to the songs she had sung at their house. There was something about those songs that made her feel happy inside, as if an angel had come to visit her.

The little girl asked Martha about the wonderful feeling at her house. Martha told the girl that it was because Somebody very special lived there. His name was Jesus.

The little girl wondered why Jesus had come to Martha's house but not to hers. She wished that He would come to live at her house too. The little girl remembered that her grandmother had taught her to pray, so she said her prayers and hoped that angels would visit her home while she slept.

At night when the little girl was alone in bed she would think about that family across the street.

Every Sunday morning Martha's family climbed into their car, and off they went to church. One Sunday the little girl and her sisters were invited to go along. Excited as little butterflies, the girls put on their prettiest dresses and scrunched into the backseat next to Martha. *Maybe this will be the place to find out about Jesus,* the little girl hoped.

Inside the church building, beautiful sounds boomed out from the organ, and everyone stood to sing like one huge choir. The sound was so wonderful that the little girl thought she must be in heaven. In Sunday school, she listened to the teacher and decided that Jesus lived there in that church too. But how could she take Him home with her? How could she tell her mom and dad about Him?

Later that day, back in the neighborhood, Mrs. Lay sat on the porch with the little girl and her sisters. "I am glad you liked church," she said with a smile. "What was your favorite part?"

"Well, my teacher hugged me and gave me my very own Bible," said the little girl. "And she said that Jesus can live in your heart. But I don't know if He wants to come into *my* heart."

The girl asked a lot of questions until finally Mrs. Lay said, "Would you like to invite Jesus to live in your heart? If you ask Him to come in, you can be sure that He will. He wants to help you grow into the person He created you to be. I will pray with you if you'd like."

The little girl spoke right up, "Oh, I'd like that very much. But what about all the hateful, ugly things I've said and done?"

Inside the church building, beautiful sounds boomed out from the organ, and everyone stood to sing like one huge choir.

"That is exactly why Jesus died on the cross," said Mrs. Lay. "All of us have ugly things in our hearts that need to be forgiven. Jesus makes you a brand-new person on the inside. Then He helps you to obey Him."

At that moment, the angels must have been swirling all around the neighborhood, for the little girl *did* pray and ask Jesus to forgive her. She didn't wait another minute. She asked Him to come and live in her heart and make her home like Martha's.

Something happened that made the girl feel very happy. She would tell you that she still wasn't perfect after that, but she *did* have a new best friend named Jesus to help her. She read her new Bible and tried to learn as much as she could. That very day, the little girl took Jesus home with her, and everyone soon noticed that she was happier and kinder than she had ever been. Every day she knelt down next to her bed and prayed that Jesus would fill her heart and her home with His love. And He did.

The girl wants you to know that Jesus can live in your house too. He is the best friend to have, because He is with you all the time. He helps you do what is kind and loving, just as if He lived right inside your heart, and He can change your whole family. The girl who told me the story hopes that you will pray and ask Jesus to forgive your sins and come to live in your heart . . . and in your home too. She

> *Every day the little girl knelt down next to her bed and prayed that Jesus would fill her heart and her home with His love.*

also hopes that you will pray for your family and for the kids in your neighborhood. And the girl said she's glad that now you know her story.

By the way, if you are wondering how I know so much about this girl, I think it's time to tell you. You see, I'm a grandmother now, but I was that little girl a long time ago.[1]

MISS BOBBIE

CHAPTER ONE

Into My Heart

When Do My Children Need to Receive Jesus as Their Savior?

But Jesus called the children to Him and said, "Let the little children come to me, and do not hinder them, for the kingdom of God belongs to such as these."
(Luke 18:16, NIV)

The scene is familiar. You have probably seen paintings depicting the tender and wonderful moment.

Jesus is teaching a group of grown-ups when a handful of kids begins to make a ruckus. The disciples, no doubt annoyed that the Master's proclamation has been interrupted, do their best to corral and quiet the children so Jesus can continue.

But Jesus disrupts the disruption. He tells the disciples to stop their complaining. Not only does He not mind the extra noise of the little ones, He surprises everyone when He invites the children to come to Him. He takes the initiative. He draws them close. But it's not the first time.

From the beginning of time . . . long before our great-great-grandparents were conceived . . . God knew us and loved us and wanted to draw us to Himself. Jesus' compelling love isn't only for our children;

it's for us as grown-ups as well. "We love Him because He first loved us" (1 John 4:19).

The adventure of leading your children to Christ begins with being aware of your own need for a Savior and the commitment of your life into His care. When you as a parent have a vibrant personal relationship with God, you can wrap your own love for Jesus around your children like a sweater on a cold day.

There's *nothing* more important for Christian parents than to spiritually nurture their kids so they can make their own profession of faith in Jesus Christ. Ultimately, however, every person, no matter his or her age, must make the decision alone to follow Christ.

> *From the beginning of time . . . long before our great-great-grandparents were conceived . . . God knew us and loved us and wanted to draw us to Himself.*

Why Do Our Children Need Jesus?

The Internal Revenue Service refers to our kids as "dependents." The idea is that while they're living in our home, our children have needs that are met by responsible grown-ups—people on whom they can *depend*. You see this when a little girl spontaneously reaches for her dad's hand when she's crossing a busy street or when a little boy runs to his mother for comfort after the neighbor kids have verbally assaulted him.

Unfortunately, the protection of our "dependents" has limitations. As parents we can watch over our children physically. We do our best to safeguard them emotionally. But spiritual rebirth is not possible for us to give.

SING TOGETHER

For thousands of years, Christ-followers have celebrated their friendship with God through the singing of hymns and spiritual songs. Profound lyrics set to beautiful melodies have provided instruction, comfort, and hope to millions of believers around the world for centuries. Hymns are a great way for you to teach your children the truths of the Christian faith.

And, of course, every weekend in church we affirm with other believers our faith in Jesus Christ through the singing of hymns and praise songs. From the time we were children, hymns have played a vital role in our Christian faith, and music became a natural way for us to teach our daughters sound theology.

After our family sang a hymn together just two or three times, Missy and Julie had it memorized. Soon we'd hear them singing the words to themselves. We knew that the words were sinking into their heart and building their character. We've had the pure delight of passing the love of hymns to our children and they, in turn, to their children. Can you imagine the fun of hearing our two-year-old granddaughter singing as she washes her hands, "What can wash away my sin? Nothing but the blood of Jesus."

Because Bobbie and I know the power of music as you introduce your children to Christ, we encourage you to use the CD of hymns that's enclosed in this book to help teach your child what it means to follow Jesus. Slip it into the CD player in your car and you'll find that after just a few short trips, your children will be singing along. You will be singing, too.

There's no need to have a concert-worthy voice. That's not important. But once these hymns are memorized, their words provide a source of great truth and inspiration.[2]

The longing in their hearts for God's forgiveness and acceptance is not ours to fulfill. The philosopher Blaise Pascal[3] called this "the God-shaped vacuum in every person's soul." This vacuum comes in every size—large, medium, and small—and it can only be filled with the presence of the heavenly Father.

Jesus called this soul-filling experience being "born again."[4] And it's interesting that He used the image of our children being welcomed into the light of day from the darkness of a mother's womb to describe the darkness of spiritual separation from Him and the light of the "new birth."

When Is the Right Time?

You and I know that selfishness and disobedience are hardwired to our children's DNA. Refusing to share toys with the neighbor toddler or disobeying our instructions happens with no coaching at all. This behavior can be credited to the sin nature that is conceived in every human being.

Spiritual rebirth is not possible for us to give.

The defining moment regarding their readiness for being born again begins when our children understand that their selfishness and misbehavior are sinful. You discover this when you see that your children have the capacity to make a choice between obedience and disobedience, between kindness and greed, between speaking harsh words and loving words. You may also recognize their readiness when you observe them feeling a sense of shame and remorse once you have punished them for doing naughty things.

BIBLES FOR EVERYONE

If you've not already done so, we encourage you to buy a Bible for everyone in your family, including the youngest kids.[5] At night before you tuck your children into bed, read from *their* Bible. If they're old enough, encourage them to read along.

God promises that His Word will provide a lifetime of light for your children's path . . . a cure for their lifelong struggle with sin.

> *How can a young man cleanse his way?*
> *By taking heed according to Your word.*
> *With my whole heart I have sought You;*
> *Oh, let me not wander from Your commandments!*
> *Your word I have hidden in my heart,*
> *That I might not sin against You. . . .*
> *Your word is a lamp to my feet and a light to my path.*
> *(Psalm 119: 9-11, 105)*

We recently heard a story about a six-year-old boy who said to his mother, "It's sad that I can talk to Jesus but He can't talk to me." This gave his mother a chance to remind her son that the Bible *is* God's way of talking to us.

The path to obedience is paved with God's Word.

We know that the state of moral awareness and spiritual accountability comes to children at different ages. We have seen our own children and grandchildren come to this place of maturity at different times . . . anywhere from about four to eight years old.

In December 2001, our granddaughter Abby, then almost six years old, was playing with her nearly four-year-old brother, Luke. It was Christmastime, and they were setting up a plastic nativity scene in their playroom. Of course, Mary, Joseph, the baby Jesus, and a handful of shepherds were huddled together with some livestock looking on. Luke had added a couple of Power Ranger action figures and the conductor of his Thomas the Tank Engine set.

Missy, our daughter, was busy in the kitchen when Luke came running downstairs with an announcement. "I a Cwistian," he said. Thinking that Luke had said, "I have a question," Missy asked her son what he wanted.

"No," Luke replied. "I a *Cwistian*!"

A linguistic expert at deciphering little-boy-ese, after hearing it a second time, his mother understood. Luke was telling her that he had invited Jesus into his heart. "Oh, Luke, that's wonderful!" Missy said. "Tell me about it."

Luke told his mom that Abby had told him she thought his action figures and train conductor didn't really belong in the manger scene because they might not be Christians.

Then Luke had confessed to his sister, "But I'm not a Cwistian either."

"Would *you* like to ask Jesus into your heart?" Abby had asked Luke.

"Yes," Luke replied. And so, with the help of his sister, he asked Jesus to come and live in his heart.

"How did you know what to do?" Missy questioned.

"I copied Abby," Luke replied.

And how did Abby learn what to pray? She had learned it from her parents, who had led her to a simple encounter with Jesus a few years before. In the same way, Jon and Missy later talked with Luke to be sure he understood what he had done.

The Bible story of Jesus and the interrupting children leaves out an important detail. Have you ever wondered just how those kids suddenly appeared in

Luke was telling her that he had invited Jesus into his heart.

the presence of the Master? Actually, there's little doubt. A parent or another grown-up brought the children to Jesus. You and I have the privilege of doing the same thing. Even though they're young, they can be brought to the Savior and made new creations. Even though they are small, they can be born again. Just like you and me.

Into My Heart

In our family, music has played a powerful role toward an understanding of God's love and grace. Music has also given us handles to teach our children an appropriate and understandable response to God's invitation to know and follow Him.

Bobbie's experience of salvation (see the introduction) as an eight-year-old was punctuated by a little song she learned at the church where her neighbor took her. Its simple lyric sealed the moment.

Into my heart, into my heart, come into my heart, Lord Jesus.
Come in today; come in to stay, come into my heart, Lord Jesus.

There are literally hundreds of references to "the heart" in the Bible. Most commonly this word is used to describe the resting place of a person's emotions. We understand this when husbands give their wives Valentine's cards beautifully designed with *heart-shaped* art. The words *I Love You* are always perfectly scripted across the front. And when the wife receives the card, she often responds to her husband, "I love you *with all my heart.*"

Sometimes heart-shaped gifts come as a symbol of contrition for hurtful actions or words thoughtlessly spoken. Following his adultery with Bathsheba and his being found out, King David wrote: "Create in me a clean *heart*, O God, and renew a steadfast spirit within me" (Psalm 51:10, italics ours).

In our family, music has played a powerful role toward an understanding of God's love and grace.

Of course, the heart David was referring to was not a box of chocolates or the fist-sized, blood-pumping muscle in the center of his chest. David was asking God to take his emotions, his "loves," and shape them in such a way that they would be drawn to Him.

When you and your child sing "Come into my heart, Lord Jesus," you are asking God to take charge of your passions. Like a great magnetic force, you want the metal shavings of your affections to be pulled in His direction.

When Moses pleaded with Pharaoh for the release of the Israelites from their Egyptian captivity, do you remember how the Scripture describes the pagan monarch? That's right—"his heart was hard." That meant that the decisions he made came from a seedbed of bitterness and hatred toward God's people.

Jesus underscored this truth when He said: "For from within, out of the *heart* of men, proceed evil thoughts, adulteries, fornications, murders, thefts, covetousness, wickedness, deceit, lewdness, an evil eye, blasphemy, pride, foolishness. All these evil things come from within and defile a man" (Mark 7:21-23, italics ours).

Like a coach on the sidelines who shouts orders to his players on the field, it's our heart that directs the words of our mouth, the actions of our hands, and the movement of our feet. So when we ask Jesus to be our Savior—to come into our hearts—we're acknowledging our helplessness, giving Him control of everything that provokes us to action.

For a six-year-old child, a changed heart will mean a renewed motivation to share his toys or the will to obey his mother or speak kindly to his sister. To a grown-up, it means saying "no" to infidelity or gossip or greed.

As you watch your children, pay close attention to their motives and the intentionality of their activity. Look for moments of contemplation . . . of willfulness or contrition or guilt. In these moments of quiet, the time may be right to tell them about their heart. Remind your child how much God loves them and wants them to have a heart that loves Him too.

My heart is steadfast, O God,
my heart is steadfast;
I will sing and give praise. (Psalm 57:7)

One Boy's Story

To Read to Your Children

My name is Luke and I am six years old. Not long ago my family celebrated a special day for my brother, Isaac, and I want to tell you about it.

Isaac is four years old and goes to preschool two days a week. One day his teacher asked the kids to make cutout letters of the alphabet at home and bring them to school for a project. I watched my mom help Isaac cut out his letters at the kitchen table. For each letter, Isaac thought of a word that begins with that letter. When they got to the letter *J*, Isaac said, "*J* is for Jesus."

"That's good, Isaac," my mom said. "Someday I hope you will invite Jesus to live in your heart."

Isaac was quiet for a minute. Then he said, "I want to invite Jesus into my heart today, Mom."

My mom asked Isaac if he knew what it meant to invite Jesus into his heart. He said that he wasn't sure, so she picked up some pieces of colored construction paper to explain it. She chose five colors: gold, black, red, white, and green. I will tell you what each color means.

Gold stands for God and for heaven, God's home. The Bible says that in heaven the streets are made of gold and no one is sick there and no one ever dies. God is holy and perfect and made heaven and earth. And God made you and me. He loves us and wants us to live with Him in heaven someday.

The black is like the darkness of sin. Sin is anything that makes God sad—things I think about or do that hurt others, like being selfish or hitting my sister. It's sin in my heart that makes me tell lies and say mean things. The Bible says everyone sins. My sins keep me away from God. But God loves me even when I do bad things. And He wants to give me a clean, new heart that doesn't have sin in it.

The red stands for Jesus' blood. God sent His Son, Jesus, to be punished for my sin. Jesus died on a cross, but on the third day, God raised Him to life again.

God loves me even when I do bad things. And He wants to give me a clean, new heart that doesn't have sin in it.

White is the color of snow, and that's how clean my heart can be. I need to tell Jesus that I am sorry for my sin and believe that He died for me.

Green is the color of grass and trees and things that grow. It reminds me that I need to grow to love God more and more. After I ask Jesus to forgive my sin, my love for God can grow strong. I can keep growing by learning about God in the Bible and going to church and praying.

When Isaac asked Jesus to come into his heart, he prayed a special prayer. My mom said a few words and then let Isaac repeat them. I remember praying like that when I invited Jesus into my heart. This is the prayer that my mom helped Isaac to pray:

"Dear God, thank You for loving me so much. Thank You for sending Jesus to die for me and take my sin away. I know I have sin in my heart. Please forgive my sin. I want to make You happy. I want my heart to be as clean and white as snow. Please come into my heart and help me love You more every day. Amen."

Because Isaac invited Jesus into his heart, we had a family celebration. This was just like we did when my sister and I invited Jesus to come into our heart. Everyone in my family makes a big deal about it because dad and mom say it's like a birthday. The person gets to pick what they want for dinner. I chose pizza—without mushrooms—on my special day, and Isaac said he wanted to go out for a cheeseburger. We call our Grammie and Papa and Granddaddy and Nanny on the phone and later we buy a new Bible.

Now everyone in my family is a Christian. Sometimes at dinner my dad asks us, "What did God say to you today?" and we each say what we think God said to us in our heart. One day I had a new set of LEGOs. All day long I thought about those LEGOs. When it was my turn to answer my dad's question, I told everyone, "God wants me to love Jesus more than my LEGOs."

God is always helping me to make wise choices and to love Him more than anything else. He can help you too.

CHAPTER TWO

Holy! Holy! Holy!

Who Is God?

*The heavens declare the glory of God;
and the firmament shows His handiwork.
(Psalm 19:1)*

The ninety-minute westward drive from Calgary to Banff, Canada, is one of our favorites. Just a few miles west of the city, the topography begins to change from tabletop flat to gently rolling plains. In forty minutes, we can see on the horizon the hint of what is to come. Less than an hour after leaving the Calgary city limits, the breathtaking panorama of the Canadian Rockies juts brazenly into the sky. With each mile the craggy peaks come into clearer focus. Until we reach the resort city of Banff, every bend in the road brings more spectacular vistas and more gasps of amazement at their grandeur.

This is wonder that has to be seen to be believed.

In matters of faith, the reverse is true. To experience the presence of an awesome God, He must be believed to be seen. Your "eyes of faith" turn the barren plain of lethargy and doubt into heart-pounding wonder. Just the thought of Him takes your breath away.

Do you remember the first moment you saw your child? That indescribable sensation when you first laid your eyes on your baby—whether through natural birth or adoption—is one that you'll never forget. This was God's blessing . . . and you knew it. You were a spectator to a miracle.

From that moment forward, in the presence of your child, that sense of wonder needs to fill your heart whenever you're reminded of God's creation, His gifts, and His love and grace. This same awe takes root in your children as they watch how His beauty and presence impacts you.

From the time our daughters were small, Missy and Julie would overhear us saying to each other, "Isn't God amazing?" It was a natural part of our lexicon when we'd be scooting along a highway and see a sunset or watching ants tromp in single file across the sidewalk in front of our house.

The first step in the process of leading your children to a personal relationship with Christ is to give them a sense of your own reverence for God. *He* is the most important person in the world to you. As your children grow and discover the truth of God's love and His provision of grace for them, they'll be familiar with Him

Your children will be familiar with God because of how you have spoken words of adoration about your heavenly Father.

because of how you have spoken words of adoration about your heavenly Father.

As Christian parents, our primary task is to demonstrate to our chil-

TEACH THEM TO PRAY

Bringing your children into God's presence through prayer is an unspeakable privilege. Teaching them to pray also gives you the opportunity to show them another way to honor the Lord.

Mealtimes and bedtimes are ideal times for prayer. By your own example, teach your child how to speak words of affirmation and gratitude to God. The younger your child, the more likely he is to thank God for unusual things, like the frog in the creek or a new box of breakfast cereal. That's okay—the older he gets, the more meaningful these "thank yous" will become.

Also teach your child to learn to ask forgiveness for specific actions. By confessing his own sin, your child will begin to understand the truth of a loving heavenly Father's forgiveness.

Then invite your child to bring his requests to the God of the universe, who is listening carefully. Like his list of "thank yous," he may have a long list of everyday requests ("Bless the garbage man, bless my Hot Wheels and Rescue Heroes, please help my T-ball team win tomorrow. . ."). Again, it's okay. Your child is learning to trust God to meet his needs.

Finally, we encourage you to help your child close the prayer by thanking God once more.

The best way for your child to learn how to pray is for them to hear you pray with them and for them. Let them hear you speak words of adoration and worship, confess your sins, make specific requests, and then thank Him again for listening and answering.[6]

dren what it literally means to stand in the presence of a holy God. And when we are filled with that awareness, everything changes.

Speechless

Take a minute to review your own experience in school. What if we were to ask you which teacher or professor or coach had the most profound impact on your life? Go ahead . . . take a second to think about the answer. What words would you use to describe this person?

Though you probably knew that the person you respected so much really cared for you, it's likely that that teacher or coach was also *tough, knowledgeable, demanding,* and *resolute.* Words like *permissive, indecisive,* and *uncertain* rarely describe the people who make an indelible impact on us.

Influential people from our past made an impression on us because of our respect for them. The Bible calls this "fear."

For children, "fear" conjures up visions of monsters lurking in the dark or thieves waiting to break into their house. But as adults we understand the power of the word in a different context. We *fear* casual attitudes about loaded guns and speeding cars on busy highways.

And as Christians we *fear* God.

Solomon, one of the wisest men in history, put it plainly: "The fear of the LORD is the beginning of knowledge" (Proverbs 1:7, NIV).

When we stop to consider the Holy One in whose presence we stand, our pulses should quicken, our knees should buckle in worship. Yes, He is our friend. Yes, He tenderly invites us to come into His presence. Yes, He loves us with unfathomable love. But He is not our buddy or chum.

He is the One who created the grandeur of those Canadian Rockies with nothing but the sound of His voice, the flawless painting of a sunset, and the microscopic instinct of the marching sidewalk ants with a single word.

This fact should send chills down our spines. It should take our breath away.

As residents of central Florida during late summer 2004, we experienced firsthand three powerful hurricanes. The "eyes" of Charley, Frances, and Jeanne passed over our county within a span of six weeks. For a total of forty-four hours during these storms we hunkered down and waited. Outside our home, sustained winds of over a hundred miles an hour snapped huge old-growth oak trees like Popsicle sticks. Inside we held our breath and wondered.

The presence of these hurricanes could not be ignored. We sat in the living room and sang hymns. We tried to read. But the power of the storms kept our pulses quick, our emotions at the ready. We were experiencing something over which we had no control—storms that could have reduced everything we own to a spread of rubble in a moment.

Influential people from our past made an impression on us because of our respect for them.

In Scripture, God's Spirit is likened to a mighty wind. "When the Day of Pentecost had fully come, they were all with one accord in one place. And suddenly there came a sound from heaven, as of a rushing mighty wind, and it filled the whole house where they were sitting" (Acts 2:1-2).

The way the people felt when the Holy Spirit descended on them must have been the same way we felt as we waited out the hurricanes. Their hearts pounded at the power and the presence of God. He was not to be challenged or debated. He was to be revered and worshipped . . . and believed.

Shedding Light on Our Sin

Several years ago, our friends George and Noreen Yowell invited us to an evening meeting in their home. They were part of our Sunday school class leadership team and this was going to be our regular quarterly get-together. The meeting was set for seven, but we didn't get the memo that it would include dinner.

Late that afternoon, we changed into our "soft clothes" and headed out for the meeting.

We arrived at the Yowells' house right on time and could tell by the cars in the driveway that the others were already there. Knocking on the door to let them know we were there, we walked in without waiting for an answer. Just to the left of the entryway was the dining room. Looking at the table, Bobbie gasped. Candles flickered, illuminating a flawless spread of linen, china, and crystal.

There stood our friends, dressed for a fancy dinner party, and there we stood, looking like we were getting ready to rake leaves.

"We're in trouble," she whispered.

As we entered the living room, her fears were confirmed. There stood our friends, dressed for a fancy dinner party, and there we stood, looking like we were getting ready to rake leaves.

We were horrified and apologized for the way we looked. Our

CONNECT WITH A LOCAL CHURCH

Another way you can teach your children to love and honor Christ is by taking them to church every week. There's a kind of ecstasy about sitting together as a family and worshipping the God you love. Your child hears your voice singing and praying and it creates a bond with Christ, His family, and with you.

Church is the place where you and your children can gain a deeper knowledge of God's Word in Sunday school and small group Bible studies. When they're older, your children may sign up for a mission trip where God's work across the world can be brought into sharp focus.

Your church is filled with other adults with whom your children will establish friendships. During those times when you and your children aren't connecting as well as you should, these "free adults" will affirm what you have taught your kids. They'll help keep your children solidly grounded in their walk with Christ.

Like "home base" when we play hide-and-seek as kids, your church is a safe place—a fortress really—that has stood firm against centuries of all kinds of warfare—visible and invisible.

Jesus said, "I will build my church, and the gates of Hades will not overcome it" (Matthew 16:18, NIV). That sounds like a good place for you and your children to hang out, doesn't it?

friends were extremely gracious and told us not to worry about it. But try as we might, for the next three hours we couldn't help but think about our tacky appearance in contrast to our dressed-up friends.

When we're in the presence of a Holy God, a profound awareness sweeps over us—an awareness of our sinfulness. We know we're in trouble. We are overwhelmed by His majesty and reminded of our sinfulness. We're invited guests at a state dinner and we've come in our workout clothes. And there's nothing we can do about it on our own.

Holy! Holy! Holy!

The prophet Isaiah knew all about being underdressed. As part of his daily routine, he would visit the Temple to pray. One morning he had a vision that changed his life. Even though Isaiah was a professional God-talker, apparently he had forgotten Who it was that he was talking about.

As the clop of his sandals echoed from the walls of the empty Temple, Isaiah suddenly heard something. He looked up and "saw the Lord." Isaiah was surrounded by a chorus of angels who sang to each other, "Holy, holy, holy is the LORD Almighty; the whole earth is full of His glory" (Isaiah 6:3, NIV).

But Isaiah did not celebrate the sights and sounds of God's presence. Isaiah was petrified that the One whose name he preached had also shown up for morning prayers. Like Bobbie and me at the dinner party, Isaiah became profoundly aware of his own fallen condition.

Woe is me, for I am undone!
Because I am a man of unclean lips,

And I dwell in the midst of a people of unclean lips;
For my eyes have seen the King,
The LORD of hosts. (Isaiah 6:5)

Do you see it? When we're in the presence of a Holy God, our sinfulness comes clearly into focus.

The same thing happened centuries later when Jesus joined His disciples on their fishing boats. "Put down your nets," He told them.

"But Master," they protested, "we've fished all night and haven't landed a single fish."

But because Jesus was Jesus, they obeyed and dropped their nets into the murky darkness of the sea. In an instant, the nets were filled with fish. Simon Peter, who should have been delighted, was filled with shame.

"Depart from me, for I am a sinful man, O Lord!" he cried, falling to his knees (Luke 5:8).

When we're in the presence of a Holy God, our sinfulness comes clearly into focus.

There it is again. Becoming aware of God's presence fills us with wonder . . . and inadequacy. His perfection shines a penetrating light on our imperfection.

What are we to do?

Thank God; He *has* provided us with an answer to this dilemma.

Who Made Thunderstorms?

To Read to Your Children

What do you do during thunderstorms? I mean the kind of rumbling storms that light up the sky and rattle the windows. *Boom! Boom! Boom!* goes the thunder. It sounds like gunshots right outside your home. The lightning flashes look like fireworks.

I know some kids who have a plan to keep from being scared by thunderstorms. Their mom and dad came up with a good idea. If you like it, you may want to do this the next time a crackling thunderstorm starts to boom in your neighborhood.

Here's what my friends do. When the thunderstorm starts to roll in, they all huddle together wherever they are—on the sofa or on the biggest bed in the house—and "snuggle" until the storm is over. At the first sounds of the frightful noises and sights, someone says, "Oh, goodie, it's time to snuggle!" Then everyone runs to the circle of hugs. All of the kids have a hand to hold and someone to be close to as they watch and listen to the storm outside.

The Bible tells us who made the skies where the storms come from. God made them. God is the One who created everything in the heavens and on the earth. He is the Lord God Almighty, the Maker of heaven and earth. The Bible says that God sends out His mighty voice and that His power is in the skies (see Psalm 68:33). And like our friends who snuggle during the thunderstorms, God also gently holds us with His love (see Deuteronomy 33:26-27). What an awesome God He is!

God lives in heaven, and besides being very powerful, He is also perfect. There is one word that means "perfect." All the angels in heaven use it over and over again as they sing about God. They say "Holy! Holy! Holy!" and they do everything God tells them to do. God wants you and me to know how great and kind He is. He wants us to reverence Him, too. That means to show respect for Him and obey Him because of how perfect and mighty and kind He is.

There is a very special hymn that helps us to sing about our perfect and wonderful God. When we sing "Holy! Holy! Holy!" we use the same word the angels do to tell God how mighty He is.

God is the One who created everything in the heavens and on the earth.

We can talk to God out loud or silently in our heart and tell Him that He is powerful and mighty and perfect. We can thank Him for all He has made and remember that He loves us. It's sort of like running to your dad or mom in a storm. When you talk to God about His love for you and your love for Him, it's like you're snuggling with Him. He wants you to know that He is strong and can keep you safe.

The next time you hear thunder or see a flash of lightning or look at the beautiful sky after the storm, remember the Lord God Almighty who created it all. Remember that He is holy and that He loves you very much.

CHAPTER THREE

What Can Wash Away My Sin?

Sin and the Cross

It was very early on a Saturday morning when we backed out of our driveway in Nashville and headed south on Interstate 65 to Birmingham. Our daughter Julie was a freshman at Samford University, and we were on our way to pick her up and then attend a special parents' luncheon sponsored by her sorority.

We pulled up in front of her residence hall right on time and there she stood on the porch waiting for us. She had only been away from home for a month but we greeted her as though it had been a year. After hugs and kisses, Julie got in the backseat and handed me printed directions to the Knights of Columbus hall where the luncheon was going to be held.

I studied the map as Bobbie and Julie filled the air with stories and laughter. The map clearly said that it should take "about fifteen minutes" to get from Samford to the hall. We were going to get there just in time.

However, for some completely unknown reason (I insisted that the map was very confusing), fifteen minutes passed and we were still driving. Twenty minutes . . . no Knights of Columbus hall.

I groaned audibly. "What's the matter, Daddy?" Julie asked.

"See those guys with chain saws, cutting up a tree?" I didn't wait for Julie to respond. "We passed them ten minutes ago."

"Are you sure?" Bobbie exclaimed in her doing-my-best-not-to-sound-too-panicked voice.

"Yes," I said softly. "I'm sure."

Julie looked at the clock on the dashboard. "We're going to be late, aren't we?"

"Yes, honey, we're lost," I confessed.

A strange mix of dread and anger filled the car. No more stories—and certainly no more laughter.

Being lost is no fun at all.

Sheep, Coins, and Kids

Jesus was addressing a group of religious folks—the Pharisees—who raised a question about His companions. The Pharisees called them "sinners"—scum of the earth. What was a man claiming to be the Messiah doing with such riffraff?

As He so often did, Jesus returned their question with a story . . . actually, in this case, three stories. To illustrate why He spent time—even ate meals—with these people who had been the outcasts of society, Jesus talked about a lost sheep, a lost coin, and a lost son. And in each of these accounts, the lost things were found, which set off celebrations all the way to heaven.

Being lost is no fun at all.

In these stories about lostness, Jesus was giving His audience a lesson about sin. Like the day we wandered around Birmingham, lostness is miserable. You don't know where you are. Nothing looks familiar. The aching feeling in the pit of your stomach is a constant reminder that things aren't right. You're so lost you can't even find your way back home, much less follow directions to where you're supposed to be going.

Adding to the graphic word picture of the consequences of sin, Jesus also called lost people, those who "walk in darkness" (John 8:12). Combine the blindfold of "darkness" with "lostness" and you have the picture of complete and utter horror. Sin is this and more.

Sin Is Universal

The Bible makes it perfectly clear that we are sinful—lost and in darkness—from the moment of our birth. "For all have sinned and fall short of the glory of God" (Romans 3:23, NIV).

Sinfulness shows up in our families every day—greed, angry outbursts, disobedience, rudeness, and selfishness. These reveal our sin nature, the part of us that Satan constantly tries to influence. Sinfulness is not simply a matter of doing bad things; it's a compelling force that draws us away from God toward darkness and misery.

The apostle Paul explained it this way: "As it is, it is no longer I myself who do it, but it is sin living in me" (Romans 7:17, NIV).

We have friends whose little girl was being particularly naughty one day. By midafternoon, in complete frustration, her mom sat down with Vickie and explained to her that our lives are in a tug-of-war between God—the One who wants us to be kind and obedient—and Satan—the

29

one who doesn't. In careful detail, Vickie's mother told her that she needed to be obedient to God and listen to her parents.

The rest of the day, Vickie was as close to perfect as a five-year-old could be. Her words were kind, she obeyed the first time, and she even shared her toys with her little brother.

But the next day was another story. From the moment Vickie woke up, it seemed as though she had completely forgotten yesterday's resolution to please God. Soon after breakfast, Vickie's mother sat down with her to ask about her pitiful behavior.

Looking at her mother, Vickie announced, "I've decided to go with the other guy."

The story makes us smile, but the reality of sin's power over our children is no laughing matter.

Sin Equals Death

The most tragic story in all of history was when Adam and Eve willfully disobeyed God. Until that moment, their surroundings were pristine and unspoiled. They felt no embarrassment about their naked bodies. But their open defiance to God's directive gave them eyes to see their nakedness so "the LORD God made tunics of skin, and clothed them" (Genesis 3:21).

Do you see what happened when Adam and Eve sinned? Someone—in this case an animal—had to die in order to cover them.

From that moment forward, death became the payment for sin. A careful reading of the rest of the Old Testament tells the story, over and over again—the need for sacrifice to cover guilt. Families brought their most perfect animal to the Temple to be killed by the priest. He would put the animal on a stone altar. He would place his hands on the head of the animal and ceremonially transfer the family's sin to its little body. Then he would kill the animal as dads and mothers and children watched.

As gruesome as this may sound, a holy God's anger over sin and the consequences of disobeying Him were serious. Justice would only be served when blood was shed. In God's eyes, sin was this terrible. "Without the shedding of blood there is no forgiveness" (Hebrews 9:22, NIV).

The sadness that families experienced knowing that their sin caused the death of something they valued—something so innocent—made an indelible impression. That was exactly the point. Sin was a very serious thing.

Jesus the Lamb

The story of Jesus going to the cross can be greatly misunderstood. Some see His execution as the consequence of a battle between the common believers and the orthodox Jewish hierarchy of the day. Others lay blame to the inept leadership of the occupying Romans. Neither of these explanations is correct.

Jesus—God's perfect Son—went to the Cross to do what animal sacrifices could not do: satisfy God's anger over the sins of the entire world in one final bloody sacrifice. John the Baptist called Jesus "the Lamb of God, who takes away the sin of the world" (John 1:29, NIV). In the book of Revelation, the apostle John referred to Jesus as "the Lamb who was slain" (5:12).

The pain that Jesus experienced on the cross was not just the excruciating suffering of death by crucifixion. In fact, except for acknowledging

His thirst, none of the words that Scripture records had anything to do with His own physical agony. He did not say anything about the crown of thorns or the nails in His hands and feet or His inability to breathe from the suffocation that was the result of this form of execution.

No. Matthew records that His first words were "My God, my God, why have you forsaken me?" (27:46, NIV). God the Father took Jesus to the Cross and allowed Him to die and descend into hell in order to reconcile lost and sinful mankind to Himself.

Before He took his last breath, Jesus said, "It is finished" (John 19:30).

Again, He was not talking about the fact that the mock trial had accomplished its goal of sending Him to His death. He was saying that His Father's anger over sin had finally been satisfied. The mission He was sent to accomplish—to be the Lamb on the altar—was completed. Finished.

The apostle Paul summarized Adam's sin and Jesus' sacrifice this way: "For as by one man's disobedience many were made sinners, so also by one Man's obedience many will be made righteous" (Romans 5:19).

An Understandable Explanation

Good friends of ours have three children. The two older children—a boy, age eight, and a girl, age six—were working in the upstairs family room. A friend had given the children a box of tiny colorful beads and string to make bracelets and necklaces. The tediousness of the bead-stringing made for plenty of quiet. Mom was downstairs, happy for the chance to be able to catch up on some reading. Suddenly there was an ear-shattering wail . . . the unmistakable scream of a six-year-old girl.

Hurrying upstairs to the rescue, Mom found out what had happened.

The children had started to string their beads at the same time. But the little girl's dexterity gave her an advantage. Soon she had threaded lots of beads. But her older brother was having a hard time. The beads didn't seem to slip onto the thread as easily as they did for his sister.

So getting up and pretending to walk out of the room to get something from his bedroom, the boy bumped into his sister, sending her beads and string flying. Accusing him of doing this on purpose, the girl began to cry.

Because mothers have the uncanny ability to cut to the truth, soon our friend extracted a confession from her eight-year-old son. He *had*, in fact, done this on purpose. His jealousy over his sister's progress had given him the idea to put a stop to the competition.

Through tears he confessed, "I try to be nice, but I keep being mean."

This gave his mother a chance to talk again about the power of sin and the love of Jesus that forgives our sin. "There's something in our hearts that makes us do hurtful things like you just did," she said. "That's when you need to stop and remember that you need help to do what is kind and right. You can't do it on your own. That's why Jesus died."

The boy embraced his mom, thankful for a clear description of what the Cross of Jesus provides.

Her son's punishment for intentionally bumping into his sister was to think of ways to serve her for a whole week—like clear her plate from the table, make her bed, and hold the car door for her on the way to school.

"There's something in our hearts that makes us do hurtful things like you just did."

PASSING ON YOUR FAITH

The best way to begin a conversation about your children's need to receive the gift of God's grace is to tell them about your own journey of faith. You can also remind them:

- How great and good their Heavenly Father is . . . how dearly He loves them;
- How much they need Jesus to forgive them for things they do that displease Him;
- How Jesus' death on the cross and resurrection from the grave saves them from their sin and Satan's power over them and brings them into a lifelong friendship with God; and
- That God loves them so much that He wants to live in their hearts and take them to heaven when they die.

By week's end, Mom was satisfied that her boy had learned his lesson.

Luke, a Reprise

In the first chapter we told you the story of our grandson Luke and how he had happily announced to his mother, "I a Cwistian."

In the days that followed, Luke's mom and dad explained to him the story of God's provision for our sin through Jesus' death on the cross. They told him about "lostness" and "darkness" and how sin made us feel awful inside. And they explained how the blood of Jesus, the Lamb, made us clean.

"What can wash away my sin?" Missy sang to her son. "Nothing but the blood of Jesus."

A few days later, Luke came to his mother with another announcement. Apparently he had needed time to process what had happened to him.

"Mom," Luke said, his voice brimming with confidence.

"Yes, Luke," his mother replied. "What is it?"

Luke looked up, a broad smile spreading across his face. "Mom," he repeated. "I white as snow."

> *Out of the mouth of babes and nursing infants*
> *You have ordained strength,*
> *Because of Your enemies,*
> *That You may silence the enemy and the avenger. (Psalm 8:2)*

The Gift of Life

To Read to Your Children

Did you know that there is over a gallon of blood inside your body? That's a lot. Of course, you and I don't think about our blood because we can't see it . . . that is, unless we fall and scrape our knee. We put a Band-Aid on the tender place until it heals.

Blood carries good things—called oxygen and nutrients—inside our body to keep us healthy. Sometimes people get very sick because their blood is weak. They need good blood to help them get well. But where can they get this good blood?

Often near a hospital there is a building with a large red cross painted on the wall. It's a place where people can give some of their blood so it can be used for sick patients. (Don't worry. When people give blood, their body makes more.)

People walking by the Red Cross building may see a big sign that says "Give Someone the Gift of Life." The hospital wants everyone to know that people who have been hurt or who are very sick need some good blood. Only blood that is clean and free from disease can be put into the patients at the hospital. With new, healthy blood, a sick person's body can fight off illness and get better.

Though most people have healthy blood, everyone's heart is filled with sin. It's as if our heart is sick. Our heart is the part of us that thinks and feels and decides to do right or wrong. The Bible says, "All have sinned and fall short of the glory of God" (Romans 3:23, NIV). So everyone needs some powerful healing blood to make their heart clean and healthy and forgiven by God.

There is a wonderful song that asks the question, "What Can Wash Away My Sin?" The answer the song gives is, "Nothing but the blood of Jesus." When Jesus died on the cross, He gave His perfect blood to make everyone clean from sin. The Bible says, "Without the shedding of blood there is no forgiveness" (Hebrews 9:22, NIV).

Only blood that is clean and free from disease can be put into the patients at the hospital.

Do you remember the sign at the Red Cross that said, "Give Someone the Gift of Life"? Jesus is the only One who can forgive our sin and give the gift of *eternal* life. He gives it to every person who believes in Him. Jesus said, "I have come that they may have life, and that they may have it more abundantly" (John 10:10). He gave His blood on the cross to make us new and keep us strong enough to follow Him even when it's hard.

Because Jesus came back to life after He died on the cross, we will come back to life after we die too. Then we will live with Him in heaven. This is the gift of eternal life. Jesus said, "My sheep listen to my voice; I know them, and they follow me. I give them eternal life, and they shall never perish; no one can snatch them out of my hand" (John 10:27-28, NIV). You can be sure that you have eternal life when you believe Jesus and ask Him to wash your heart clean with His perfect blood. And He will never leave you.

The next time you see a cross on a building, on jewelry, or anywhere else, remember that Jesus is the only one who can give the gift of everlasting life. The song "What Can Wash Away My Sin?" tells the truth. Just like the hospital knows that you need good blood to live on this earth, God knows that nothing but the blood of Jesus can make it possible for us to live forever in heaven.

CHAPTER FOUR

The Resurrection of Jesus from the Grave

History's Greatest Victory

Jesus and His disciples were in an area called Perea, east of the Jordan River. He and His closest followers had escaped to this rural area from hostile religious leaders in Judea who had threatened to arrest Jesus for calling them blasphemers.

Miles away, in the town of Bethany, not far from where Jesus and His disciples had just fled, one of Jesus' closest friends, a man named Lazarus, became sick. Mary and Martha, Lazarus's sisters, sent word to Jesus that their brother was gravely ill.

But instead of hurrying to Bethany, Jesus stayed in Perea for two more days. This confused His disciples, who knew of His love for Lazarus. Jesus assured them that He knew what He was doing. After two days, Jesus announced, "Let us go back to Judea" (John 11:7, NIV).

Then Jesus added, "Lazarus is dead, and for your sake I am glad I was not there, so that you may believe. But let us go to him" (John 11:14-15, NIV).

Can you imagine how perplexing these words must have been for the disciples—how difficult they were to understand? But as they had many times before, with obedient faith they gathered up their belongings and followed the Master.

Two days later, as Jesus and His disciples approached the town of Bethany, a grief-stricken Martha came running to meet Him. "Lord, if You had been here, my brother would not have died," she cried. A little while later Mary came to Jesus as well. Her complaint was exactly the same.

"Where have you buried Lazarus?" Jesus asked.

The sisters led Jesus to the grave, a cave with a large stone that covered the opening.

"Take away the stone," Jesus ordered.

"But Jesus," Martha argued, "Lazarus has been dead four days. There will be a terrible smell."

"I'm doing this so you will see the glory of God," Jesus answered.

Several men rolled the stone away. Then Jesus looked toward the heavens and held court with His Father. "Father, I thank You that You have heard Me. I knew that You always hear Me, but I said this for the benefit of the people standing here, that they may believe that You sent Me" (John 11:41-42, NIV).

"Lord," Martha said to Jesus, "if You had been here, my brother would not have died" (John 11:21, NIV).

And then, staring into the darkness of the grave, Jesus commanded, "Lazarus, come forth!"[7]

The next thing the stunned crowd saw was their friend Lazarus, shuffling to the mouth of the cave, bound like a mummy in strips of cloth.

The gathered crowd was amazed and speechless. A man who had been dead four days was standing in front of them, very much alive. Can you imagine the electricity of that moment—what it must have been like, not only for Lazarus but for his family and his friends?

Life over Death, Found over Lost

Jesus raising Lazarus from the grave was only the beginning. This wouldn't be the last time that death would be conquered.

Once Jesus had "finished" His assignment on the cross, He walked out of His *own* tomb. What Jesus did in commanding Lazarus to "come forth," God the Father did for His Son.

"Jesus," God decreed. "Come forth!"

And Jesus did. He defeated death, the greatest enemy of all.

What this means for you and your children is that your sin is completely forgiven because of Jesus' death on the cross. Your life can be abundantly restored by the empty tomb. Because of Jesus' completed work, you are welcomed into the very throne room of the Creator of the universe.

Access

Have you ever tried to log on to a Web site only to realize you've forgotten your password? You enter what you think is your password and a bothersome message pops onto your screen. "Access Denied" it brashly announces. You know the sinking feeling, don't you?

God's password, the one that grants us permanent access into His presence, is "J-e-s-u-s." It was the death and resurrection of Jesus, God's perfect Lamb, that completed the final blood sacrifice. Our sin separated us from God, but He provided a way for our relationship to be restored. We can be thoroughly reconciled.

Let Me Count the Ways

Like sunlight streaming through the prisms of a multifaceted stone, the resurrection of Jesus refracts a mosaic of radiant beauty to our life. Like the bottom line of a successful financial portfolio, the dividends are many.

> *Because of Jesus' completed work, you are welcomed into the very throne room of the Creator of the universe.*

Because the consequence of our sin is always death, Jesus' victory over the grave gives us life, both earthly and eternally. Jesus made that clear when He said, "The thief does not come except to steal, and to kill, and to destroy. I have come that they may have life, and that they may have it more abundantly" (John 10:10).

In the last chapter we talked about being lost in sin. In our lostness, Jesus is precise and understandable directions: "I am the way, the truth, and the life. No one comes to the Father except through Me" (John 14:6).

We also talked about our sin encircling us in thick darkness. Even as we are surrounded by night, He is the illumination of our path: "I am the light of the world. He who follows Me shall not walk in darkness, but have the light of life" (John 8:12).

The apostle Paul, who was so adept at helping us to better understand the gift of salvation through the cross and the resurrection of Jesus

Christ, said it this way: "I have been crucified with Christ; it is no longer I who live, but Christ lives in me; and the life which I now live in the flesh I live by faith in the Son of God, who loved me and gave Himself for me" (Galatians 2:20).

Do you see it? Our sins were buried *with* Jesus when He died and was laid in the tomb. And our life *in* Him—free from the clutches of sin—is possible because that same tomb is empty.

If you've ever seen someone baptized by immersion, you may have heard the minister say something like this: "Buried with Christ," as he dips the person down into the water and "Raised to newness of life," as he lifts him out. Here's a perfect metaphor for what happens to us because of Jesus.

Going It Alone

In 1986, when our daughter Julie was twelve, she was admitted to the hospital for major surgery. For reasons that were never satisfactorily diagnosed, she was born with a "drop foot." Doctors at Vanderbilt Children's Hospital were going to transfer five tendons across her foot to allow her some limited range of motion.

We took her to her assigned room late one afternoon for a series of pre-op procedures and stayed with her throughout the night. Dr. Neil Green, one of Nashville's premier orthopedic surgeons, visited with us. In addition to giving us a rundown of what he was going to do in the operation, he also comforted us with words of assurance. His natural wit and sense of humor showed up when he pulled a permanent marker out of his pocket and wrote "Nyet," Russian for "No," on Julie's "good foot."

"Tomorrow morning I may be a little sleepy," he joked. "I don't want to operate on the wrong foot!"

Early the next morning, a nurse came in to wake us up, then she gave Julie medication to make her drowsy.

We stood by Julie's bed and prayed with her as her eyes grew heavy. When the surgical nurse came to our room and put Julie on a gurney, we asked her if we could walk along. She said that would be fine.

Walking down the hall, we held our daughter's hand as the gurney moved toward the elevator. We were silent. The squeak of the nurse's shoes on the slick floor and the flutter of the gurney's wheels were the only audible sounds. Once we were safely inside the huge elevator, the nurse selected the surgical floor and down we went. Together.

We stood by Julie's bed and prayed with her as her eyes grew heavy.

But as the doors opened and the nurse wheeled Julie to the double doors marked "Surgery: Authorized Personnel Only" she stopped. "I'll take Julie from here," she told us.

We leaned over and kissed our precious sixth grader on the forehead. "Good-bye, Julie," each of us said to her. "We love you."

The nurse gave us a reassuring smile and pushed the gurney away. The double doors snapped open like obedient soldiers, then closed as Julie disappeared behind them.

Until this moment, we were at her side. But now we couldn't go with her.

When the apostle Paul tells us that we are "crucified with Christ," he is telling us—and our children—that this is something we must do . . . alone.

Although our heart is torn as we stand back and watch our children face the need for their own experience of forgiven sin and restoration with the Father, we cannot take them the whole way to their own experience of the cross and empty tomb. This is a place they must go alone.

We can "walk alongside them" as we talk about our own personal experience of God's grace. And we can "walk alongside them" by creating an environment where God's Word is taught and Jesus is honored. But the decision to believe in Christ and follow Him is our children's alone to make.

Once again, the apostle Paul describes this miracle in understandable language: "If anyone is in Christ, he is a new creation; old things have passed away; behold, all things have become new" (2 Corinthians 5:17).

The decision to believe in Christ and follow Him is our children's alone to make.

Can you feel the joy? There is no greater delight than to see our kids burst back through those double doors . . . forgiven, clean, healed.

The Miracle of the Cross

It's common for kids to count on the strength of others to bolster their own confidence. "My daddy's bigger than your daddy," you might hear your son call to the neighborhood bully.

But as parents, we admit to our kids that even we as moms and dads aren't mighty enough to pay for our own sins, much less their misdeeds.

The lyric of "Jesus Loves Me," the first Christian song that many children learn, is profound: "They are weak but He is strong." This isn't a

PRAYING TO RECEIVE CHRIST

Though we cannot accept salvation *for* our children, we can help them understand how to grab hold of salvation once they recognize their need for Christ and express their desire to come to Him. Some parents take their children through this step by praying with them. My mother did this with me when I received Christ as a small boy. She prayed a prayer on my behalf, one phrase at a time, which I repeated after her. It went something like this:

> *Dear heavenly Father, thank You for loving me. I know that I am a sinful boy and need You to save me. Thank You for dying on the cross for me and for rising from the dead. I receive Your gift of forgiveness; thank You for Your promise to live in my heart for the rest of my life. And thank You for listening to me when I talk to You and for the promise that You will take me to heaven when I die. Amen.*

Whether you help them with the words or give them enough information so they can come to Christ with their own prayer, the important thing is that they sincerely speak words of gratitude, repentance, acknowledgment of God's grace, and acceptance and thanks for His promises. "If you confess with your mouth that Jesus is Lord and believe in your heart that God raised him from the dead, you will be saved. For with the heart one believes and is justified, and with the mouth one confesses and is saved" (Romans 10:9-10, ESV).

statement about physical strength; it's *spiritual* truth. It means that Jesus' death and resurrection conquered Satan and the sin he peddles—something even the strongest daddy can't do. "For the wages of sin is death, but the free gift of God is eternal life through Christ Jesus our Lord" (Romans 6:23, ESV).

Jesus removes your sin. That's powerful. Jesus' power also saves us from the harassment of Satan, the evil one who relentlessly haunts us and tries to lead our heart astray. That's more than we can comprehend.

Jesus' death and His resurrection from the grave seals our relationship with God, our heavenly Father, forever. Because of Jesus, our children can have a lifetime of access to the Father. That's the miracle of the Cross and the empty tomb.

The Happiest Day Ever

To Read to Your Children

Jesus knew that He had important work to do for God, His Father in heaven. He knew that He was going to die for the sins of all the people in the world so they would be able to live with God someday. That was hard for His friends to understand, so He kept telling them not to be afraid, but to trust Him. He said, "Let not your hearts be troubled. Believe in God; believe also in Me" (John 14:1, ESV).

Jesus also told His friends that after He died He would not stay dead. He knew He would come to life again. He said anyone who believes in Him will also live again in heaven. He didn't want His friends to worry. Jesus said, "I will not leave you as orphans; I will come to you. Before long, the world will not see me anymore, but you will see me. Because I live, you also will live" (John 14:18-19, NIV).

After Jesus died on the cross, His body was laid in a grave. It was like a cave inside a big rock and it was called a tomb. The disciples were very sad that their best friend, Jesus, had died. They forgot that Jesus had said He would come back to life. That's probably because they didn't understand, so they didn't really believe Him. When a body is dead, it doesn't look like it could ever live again.

But Jesus did come back to life. That was called Jesus' resurrection, and it was the happiest day ever! It happened on a Sunday morning long ago. The ground trembled with a force greater than a mighty earthquake. Jesus walked right out of the grave, alive! A dazzling angel told some of His friends not to worry. The angel said, "Do not be afraid, for I know that you seek Jesus who was crucified. He is not here, for He has risen, as He said" (Matthew 28:5-6, ESV).

Most of Jesus' close friends were meeting together in a house on that Sunday. In the evening Jesus surprised them and walked right into the room. He stood there, showing His friends that He was alive! They couldn't believe it. Jesus told them to look at His hands and feet so they would know it was really Him. He ate some food so they'd know He wasn't a ghost. He was real, and He was really alive!

Everyone began telling their friends about the Resurrection. That's how the Christian faith started spreading all over the world. Before Jesus went back to heaven, He told His friends to keep letting people know that He was alive and would never leave them. He said, "Go and make disciples of all nations, baptizing them in the name of the Father and of the Son and of the Holy Spirit, and teaching them to obey everything I have commanded you. And surely I am with you always, to the very end of the age" (Matthew 28:19-20, NIV).

Sunday, the first day of the week, is the day when Jesus came back to life. That's why so many churches hold services on Sundays. We go to celebrate Jesus' resurrection. Jesus lives. That's why we read the Bible and pray in Jesus' name. We know He is alive and hears us.

We can tell our friends about God's mighty power and the Resurrection. We can tell them that they can live forever in heaven with Jesus.

Yes, it was the happiest day ever when Jesus came to life again!

CHAPTER FIVE

I Have Decided to Follow Jesus

The Gift of Salvation

During the early eighties, we lived with our two young daughters in central Texas. As Christmas 1982 approached, Bobbie and I started planning and plotting what we'd like to give Missy and Julie.

"I think it's time that we retire their hand-me-down, garage-sale-quality bicycles," I suggested. "Let's get them brand-new bikes."

Bobbie agreed that this would be the Christmas for bicycles.

Over the next few weeks we scoped out local sporting-goods stores to find just the right bikes for our kids. We settled on an apple red one for Missy and a royal blue one for Julie. After making our purchase, we hid the bikes in the neighbor's garage.

Neither of us slept very well on Christmas Eve. The anticipation of the look on the girls' faces when they saw their new bikes kept our hearts racing all night. Earlier that day, I had relocated the bikes to the guest room—aka Santa's workshop—so they were ready to be brought into the living room.

The following morning, at just the right moment, we wheeled the bicycles into the living room. There were squeals of excitement and peals of joy like you cannot imagine. As the girls oohed and aahed over their shiny new bikes, tears of delight streamed down our faces. It was a morning we'd never forget.

A Gift That Cannot Be Earned

You probably have a story like ours . . . an unforgettable memory of the time you gave something very special to someone you love. Like our "bicycle Christmas," you remember how it felt—the great sense of satisfaction and pure pleasure—when you saw the look on his or her face.

Have you ever thought about what the recipient did to earn your gift? Perhaps you've never thought about it this way, but what did he or she do to obligate you to give the gift?

This idea may be a little distasteful to you. Why? Because a gift is something that *cannot* be earned. It is given wholly by the choice of the giver and received by someone with a thankful heart. "Oh, you didn't have to do this," the person might say when handed the beautifully wrapped package. That's exactly the point, isn't it?

"Oh, but I really *wanted* to," you respond.

The salvation that Jesus offers is a gift to be received. And there is absolutely nothing we can do to earn it.

This idea has troubled people for centuries. Religious perfectionists have made their lists of righteous activities and attitudes—dos and don'ts—that are intended to demonstrate their fitness before a holy God. Their sincerity and hard work can be quite admirable. "You're such a good person," they hope God will say. "Here's the gift of salvation."

But the gift that Jesus offers is so incredible, so immeasurable, so unfathomable, that there is nothing that we can do to earn it . . . or deserve it. Nothing.

Like the bikes the girls received that Christmas morning, salvation is a gift we cannot earn, a blessing we cannot pay for.

A Double Gift

Even though the temperature outside was only in the midforties, our daughters were riding their new bicycles up and down the street within minutes of receiving them. They had no problem knowing just what bikes do, so you know what they did with them for the next few hours. They rode them.

The gift of salvation isn't as tangible as a shiny bicycle. We can't tuck a gift card under the ribbon wrapped around it. We can't ride it up and down our street. We can't even see it, but the excitement of the new birth is even greater than the sparkle of any Christmas present. Receiving this gift takes faith . . . faith to understand and faith to believe.

> *Salvation is a gift we cannot earn, a blessing we cannot pay for.*

In His great mercy, God understood this dilemma, so He gave us a double gift: the gift of salvation *and* the gift to be able to receive it.

Once again the apostle Paul makes this truth understandable for us. "For by grace you have been saved through faith, and that not of yourselves; it is the gift of God, not of works, lest anyone should boast"(Ephesians 2:8-9).

We know that God's grace in the form of His Son—coming to earth, living, dying, and rising from the dead—is a gift. But the ability—the faith—to believe this truth is *also* a gift. Our Father knows that we need special "eyes" to see our new bicycles, so He gives us the gift of faith.

Even in their youngest years, kids are blessed with a simple and clear understanding of this gift. A mom told Bobbie that soon after her young son Daniel asked Jesus into his heart, he knew with absolute confidence that Jesus was with him wherever he went. Running into the kitchen after playing hard one summer afternoon, Daniel stood breathless. He put his hand on his chest. Feeling his heart pounding, he looked down at his shirt. "Well, helloooo Jesus!" As Daniel ran out the back door for more play, his mother smiled with the reminder of the purity and simplicity of her son's faith.

Help Me to See

During Jesus' ministry, a father brought his young son to the Master. The boy was possessed by a demon that caused him to fall into violent convulsions.

"Have compassion on us and help us," the desperate dad said to Jesus.

"If you can believe," Jesus said, "all things are possible to him who believes."

"Lord, I believe," the father responded. And then, realizing that this bold statement belied his deep uncertainty and fear, he added, "Help my unbelief!" (Mark 9:22-24).

Because he had heard of Jesus' healing power, this dad brought his son to the Savior to receive the gift of healing. But when Jesus asked about the man's faith, he knew that he needed help. So in that moment of truth the sick child's father asked for the second gift—the gift of belief.

We Have Decided

The decision to receive the gift that Jesus gives is a monumental one. Just as your "I do" at the marriage altar was life-changing, so this choice makes everything different, even for a child.

The hymn says, "I have decided to follow Jesus . . . no turning back, no turning back." But because God provides both the gift and the ability to believe, the hymn writer would have been even more accurate if he had written, "*We* have decided to follow Jesus." The Holy Spirit joins us in making this decision.

The apostle John, also called "the disciple whom Jesus loved," expressed this truth plainly and precisely: "As many as received [Jesus], to them [Jesus] gave the right to become children of God, to those who believe in His name: who were born, not of blood, nor of the will of the flesh, nor of the will of man, but of God" (John 1:12-13).

The Holy Spirit joins us in making the decision to follow Christ.

Here is this wonderful truth again . . . the *double* gift of salvation includes "the right to become children of God" *and* "the ability to believe."

Parties in Heaven and on Earth

In chapter 3 we mentioned the Gospel account of the three lost things: a sheep, a coin, and a wayward son. Jesus told those who were listening that day that these lost things represent lost people. And He said that when these lost people are found, there's a celebration in heaven.

When you invited Jesus to come into your heart, there was a great angel party. Perhaps banners with your name printed on them were unfurled.

CELEBRATE YOUR CHILD'S DECISION

If salvation is important enough to God that He asks His angels to throw a party, you can do the same. We encourage parents of young children to celebrate when their kids come to Jesus—by making a phone call to tell grandparents or a special Christian friend; buying a new Bible and writing their child's name and "new birth date" in the front. You may want to let your child choose a special place for dinner—or his favorite meal at home. These are ways to make the experience memorable, setting it apart like you do the child's physical birthday.

Like the angels did when the shepherd found his lost sheep, the woman found her lost coin, and the waiting father welcomed his lost son, you can rejoice because the *lost* has been *found*. That's reason enough to celebrate!

Jesus said it like this, "I say to you, there is joy in the presence of the angels of God over one sinner who repents" (Luke 15:10).

The same will happen when your child comes to an understanding of his or her sinfulness and receives—through the power of God's Holy Spirit—the gift of salvation.

Leigh Swanson, our pastor's wife, told us that when her son John David was three-and-a-half years old, he showed an unusual sensitivity to spiritual things. He listened to his parents and the Bible stories they read to him with keen interest. One Sunday morning, his dad had left for early church and Leigh was getting John David ready to go. He looked up at her and said, "Can a little boy ask the big Jesus into his heart?"

"Yes," his mother answered. "Would you like to?"

John David responded, "Yes, Mom."

So Leigh stopped what she was doing and prayed with her young son to receive Jesus as his Savior. Even at a very young age, God's Spirit speaks to children, eagerly drawing their hearts to Himself.

Bring Them Up

In giving instructions to fathers, the apostle Paul uses an important word. He says that parents should bring up their children "in the discipline and instruction of the Lord" (Ephesians 6:4, ESV). He didn't tell parents to "send" their kids to someone who would teach them about salvation or even "drop off" their children in front of the church where they could learn about salvation. His admonition that we "bring" them might suggest that we come along. In fact, we could even propose that Paul meant that, in matters of faith, parents should go first. "Come along," we are saying to our children. "This is how you do it."

In the first century, Paul and his friend Silas were imprisoned because they were preaching the good news of Jesus—the Cross, the Resurrection, and salvation. Late one night, a huge earthquake rocked the ground, throwing the prison doors open and even loosening the men's shackles. When the jailer realized that he had lost control of his charges, he pulled out his sword and prepared to kill himself.

Paul and Silas stopped him, assuring him that they had not escaped. The jailer was overwhelmed by the witness of these great men. He fell to his knees and asked what he needed to do to be saved. "They replied, 'Believe in the Lord Jesus, and you will be saved—you and your household' " (Acts 16:31, NIV).

When the jailer realized that he had lost control of his charges, he pulled out his sword and prepared to kill himself.

Because of Paul and Silas' faithfulness, the jailor received the gift of salvation for himself and then saw his family accept the gift too.

Parents who go first have the privilege of inviting their children to follow along.

If you confess with your mouth that Jesus is Lord and believe in your heart that God raised Him from the dead, you will be saved. For with the heart one believes and is justified, and with the mouth one confesses and is saved. (Romans 10:9-10, ESV)

Lost and Found

To Read to Your Children

Have you ever been lost and unsure what to do? Something we saw the other day reminded us how sad it is to be lost. At a store in my town, we were surrounded by a crowd of busy shoppers. Standing near the checkout counter was a little boy with dark brown hair who looked about five years old. Big tears rolled down his face as he stood on his tiptoes searching for his mother. He couldn't see her anywhere. No longer trying to act brave, the boy started sobbing so loudly that several shoppers took notice and bent down to talk to him.

"What's your name?" one kind lady asked. Of course he knew his name, but the boy was crying so hard he couldn't speak. He was lost and didn't know what to do.

Just then, the boy's mom pushed her way through the crowd saying, "Oh, there you are! I was looking for you, Conner! I've been looking everywhere for you." Conner squeezed his arms tightly around his mom's neck as she hugged him close. A big smile came across his face. And it didn't take any time to wipe away Conner's tears after that big hug.

Then Conner took his mom's hand, and they walked through the busy store together. The little boy was so happy to be with his mom that he decided he would hold her hand and not wander off again to see anything, no matter how interesting it looked. He would stay right next to his mom and make sure he followed her everywhere she went.

Jesus is a lot like the mom who came to find Conner. Jesus loves His children and doesn't want them to be lost. He wants His children near Him all day and all night. The song "I Have Decided to Follow Jesus" is a great one to sing when you have made a decision to hold on tightly to everything you have learned about Jesus, the Savior of the world. He came looking for you to tell you that He loves you and wants you to stay close to Him in your heart. You can make up your mind to hold on to every word He says in the Bible. You can decide to follow Him every day by believing that He is God's Son and by doing what pleases God.

Conner squeezed his arms tightly around his mom's neck as she hugged him close.

When you decide to be one of Jesus' followers, you will notice that His Holy Spirit helps you to make wise choices. With God's words in your heart, you will remember what to do, how to act, and what to say.

If bad things come your way or you are tempted to do something wrong, you will be able to sing, "I have decided to follow Jesus!" And you can ask Jesus to help you keep following Him as you sing the words, "No turning back, no turning back."

CHAPTER SIX

Trust and Obey

Walking with Jesus Takes Both

Although we haven't seen one of these for a long time, a fixture on every playground when we were kids was a seesaw—a teeter-totter. This was a long flat board, resting its middle across a strong steel pipe. At each end of the board was a handle and a seat.

The seesaw worked when two children sat down on opposite seats, providing a perfect balance for the board across the steel pipe. Then the children would push with their feet and go up and down, sending their friend on the other end in the opposite direction. When it was done properly, this was great fun.

Unfortunately this game wasn't without the potential for danger. Sometimes mischievous children would slide off the end of the board when their partner was on the high end, sending them to the ground with a painful thud. (No doubt this is why we don't see teeter-totters anymore.)

Using this image, we can envision two important concepts that perfectly balance our spiritual teeter-totter. These words are "trust" and "obey."

Trust

A wedding ceremony is a profound, personal experience of trust in action. Whether a couple dated for five years or five months, they both had arrived at the decision that getting married was what they wanted to do. During the courtship, they learned as much as they could about one another. They observed how the other reacted under stress or disappointment or failure. They were enamored with their betrothed's delightful sense of humor. And they loved the way he or she loved them.

So the conversation moved toward making the relationship permanent. Close friends and parents were consulted. The date was set and the detailed plans were put in motion.

However, as the clock wound down to the vow-exchanging moment in front of the church, the couple probably experienced some anxious thoughts and last-minute jitters. "Am I sure this is the right decision?" they may have wondered. "Is this the right person?"

But they pushed through their anxiety and apprehension. They went ahead with the plan and committed themselves to one another in front of a smiling congregation. And they hurried out of the church to spend the rest of their lives together.

Marriage is a profound experience of faith. Of trust. The couple did their best to make sure of their decision. It seemed right. It felt right. So they took the plunge. But where was the guarantee that this was going to work out as they had planned? What if the other person, during the courtship, had hidden something that would someday surface and crush them? What if the tenderness with which he or she had been treated was just a scheme?

There were no guarantees, were there? This wasn't something they had bought from a store with a liberal returns policy. What they "bought" was theirs. Forever.

Unlike imperfect human relationships, you and your child's walks with Jesus are grounded in a trustworthy and perfect God. You examine the truth of His claims. You think over and pray about your decision to follow Him. God's Holy Spirit confirms the decision and assures you that His promises are true. So you take the plunge.

Because of God's promises in the Bible and the urging of God's Spirit,

Marriage is a profound experience of faith.

you have great confidence in this decision. "In Him you also trusted, after you heard the word of truth, the gospel of your salvation; in whom also, having believed, you were sealed with the Holy Spirit of promise, who is the guarantee of our inheritance until the redemption of the purchased possession, to the praise of His glory" (Ephesians 1:13-14).

Along with the apostle Paul, your assurance is well founded and strong. "For I am persuaded that neither death nor life, nor angels nor principalities nor powers, nor things present nor things to come, nor height nor depth, nor any other created thing, shall be able to separate us from the love of God which is in Christ Jesus our Lord" (Romans 8:38-39).

But let's be honest. Even though part of God's gift to us is the ability to believe, this is not that shiny new bicycle that we wheeled into the living room on Christmas morning. This relationship is a matter of having confidence in something we cannot see with earthly eyes, assurance in something we cannot touch, and certainty in something we cannot hear with physical ears.

So including expressions of your own love and reverence for God—spontaneously saying things like "Isn't God amazing," like we talked about in the second chapter, singing hymns and praise songs, reciting Scripture, praying together—will make Him more tangible and more real in your home. God's Word reminds us to "Be filled with the Spirit, addressing one another in psalms and hymns and spiritual songs, singing and making melody to the Lord with all your heart, giving thanks always" (Ephesians 5:18-20, ESV).

God uses our words of gratitude to Him to build our faith and trust. Our relationship with Jesus is based on trust. Actually, trust is a requirement. "Without faith it is impossible to please Him, for he who comes to God must believe that He is, and that He is a rewarder of those who diligently seek Him" (Hebrews 11:6).

> *God uses our words of gratitude to Him to build our faith and trust.*

The seat at one end of our seesaw is trust. Once we have confessed our sin and invited Christ to live in us, He will not take our salvation away. By the power of His grace, we have placed our lives in His hands and nothing can come between us. Jesus says: "My sheep listen to my voice; I know them, and they follow me. I give them eternal life, and they shall never perish; no one can snatch them out of my hand. My Father, who has given them to me, is greater than all; no one can snatch them out of my Father's hand" (John 10:27-29, NIV).

Obey

Our seesaw is in balance because at the other end is "obey." Let's look at what can be a confusing or difficult issue for some people.

In chapter 5 we said that there is nothing we can do to earn our salvation. The gift that Jesus offers is absolutely free. It's so incredible, so immeasurable, so unfathomable, that there is nothing that we can do to earn it . . . or deserve it. Nothing.

As worthy as we try to be, we will never be good enough to merit His grace. It's a gift that cannot be won.

So why is "obey" on the other end of the seesaw? If our relationship with Jesus is so secure, why would our conduct—our obedience—be important?

Let's take a quick visit back to our conversation about the wedding ceremony. What if, once a couple had taken their vows, recessed to the back of the church, and celebrated with their friends at the reception, the bride and groom had gone back to their parents' homes or their own apartments? Even though each had promised to love, honor, and cherish "until death," they both decided that they had no interest in setting up housekeeping together.

What if the wedding ceremony hadn't changed anything?

You're ahead of us, aren't you . . . and you're right. If wedding vows mean what they say, then everything changes, including where people live.

In your new relationship with Jesus, everything changes. Your conduct is different because of what you've done. It's a natural result. "Obey" and "trust" are in perfect balance. "If anyone is in Christ, he is a new creation; old things have passed away; behold, all things have become new" (2 Corinthians 5:17).

Although obedience–doing good things–cannot save you, your obedience to God *demonstrates*–proves–that you *have* been saved.

Jesus said it this way: "If you love Me, keep My commandments" (John 14:15).

Do you see the connection? Because I love God I *want* to keep His commandments . . . I *want* to trust and obey. And in return, His love for me draws me to obedience: "The love of Christ compels us" (2 Corinthians 5:14).

The words of the hymn "Trust and Obey" give us encouragement for faith and conduct, and help us to discover the magnificent balance of trusting and obeying.

When we walk with the Lord in the light of His Word,
What a glory He sheds on our way!
While we do His good will, He abides with us still,
And with all who will trust and obey.

Trust and obey, for there's no other way
To be happy in Jesus, but to trust and obey.[8]

Sin's Warning Lights

When you buy a brand-new car, it usually takes awhile before warning lights on your dashboard–like the one that says "Service Engine Soon"–

MEMORIZING SCRIPTURE

One way to strengthen your children's ability to trust and obey is to help them memorize important Scripture verses. Their brains are like wet cement, and the verses they learn will be pressed on their hearts forever.

An easy way to help them memorize a passage is to write a verse out on an index card and then look for chances to repeat it, phrase by phrase, to your kids. Riding in the car on the way to school or sitting around the breakfast table are perfect chances for you to work on your verse together.

You can even turn the process into a game. A great verse to start with is Philippians 4:13: "I can do all things through Christ who strengthens me."

One day Bobbie took a neighbor boy named Ben on a walk. "Let's do a Bible-verse game," she said playfully. "I'll say the verse and emphasize the first word, then you say it and emphasize the second word. Then I'll do the third, and we'll keep going until we finish it."

Bobbie started: "*I* can do all things through Christ who strengthens me."

Then it was Ben's turn: "I *can* do all things through Christ who strengthens me."

"I can *do* all things through Christ who strengthens me," Bobbie responded.

Back and forth they continued until they had finished. One time around the block and Ben had it down.

When kids are struggling with doubt or temptation, the Holy Spirit can use His own Words, which they've memorized, to strengthen their faith and resolve.[9]

come on. But after miles of travel and years of use, eventually they blink their admonition.

When a couple gets married, there's a euphoria that carries the relationship for a while. But at some point life turns mundane and problems emerge.

The same is true in your walk with Christ. Trust and obey don't only need to be there when you move in together after the honeymoon, they must stay in balance for the rest of your life.

And once again, just as He did in giving you the gift of faith, God is continuing His work in your heart, day after day, year after year, giving you the power to obey Him. "For it is God who works in you to will and to act according to his good purpose" (Philippians 2:13, NIV).

God's work in your life—through the power of the Holy Spirit—is fueled with lots of endurance. He's living in you for the long haul. And His work in you not only impacts your conduct but changes your desires too.

It may mean turning off the television or changing the channel when something that violates your sensitivity to impurity appears. It may mean glancing away from provocative magazine covers at the grocery checkout or changing the subject when someone begins to gossip.

The Holy Spirit is living in you for the long haul.

Do we still sin? Unfortunately, yes. But now, because we belong to Christ, sin's warning light flashes on the dashboard of our hearts. Our disobedience cannot be ignored. We are drawn back to God, we repent, and we receive God's forgiveness.

Trust is a natural result of obedience, just as obedience follows trust.

Morning by Morning

Have you ever gone to bed with a heavy heart? Your physical exhaustion is compounded by an endless sequence of problems and failures. But in the dawn of the next morning's light, you feel refreshed. New. Ready to tackle another day.

This I recall to my mind, therefore I have hope.
Through the LORD's mercies we are not consumed,
Because His compassions fail not.
They are new every morning;
Great is Your faithfulness.
"The LORD is my portion," says my soul,
"Therefore I hope in Him!" (Lamentations 3:21-24)

Your salvation is only the beginning. God's grace is available to you every time you confess your sin, affirm His promises, and ask Him for His strength. His compassion is new every morning.

This is truth that you have the opportunity to model in front of your children. They understand the power of sin, discouragement, and isolation. Their tender hearts long to be new again too. So with God's grace firmly planted in your life, you encourage them with His promises.

When our daughter's children were toddlers, she knelt by the sofa with her children after breakfast and prayed this prayer: "Lord, I want to be a good Mommy today, but I can't do it on my own. I need your help. Please fill me today with your love and strength. And Abby wants to be a good sister today, but she can't do it on her own either. Please

73

help her today to listen to Your voice in her heart and obey You. And Luke and Isaac want to be good brothers today, but they can't do it on their own. Please help them to be strong and to obey You. Amen."

Morning by morning, in the presence of her children, Missy was affirming her confidence and trust in God's faithfulness, then she was asking Him to help each child to obey.

Anytime . . . Anywhere

Your children will become more confident of God's compassion toward them when they understand that He is always with them. One of the best ways to remind them of God's presence is to carry on a regular habit of speaking with Him as a family. When our girls were small, we dubbed several roads in our town "prayer roads."

> *Your children will become more confident of God's compassion toward them when they understand that He is always with them.*

When we were driving to church on Sunday mornings, the stretch of Franklin Road just north of Old Hickory Road was our prayer road. We would stop whatever we were talking about and begin a conversation with our heavenly Father. We'd ask Him to bless our minister and our Sunday school teachers. We would ask Him to speak to us in worship and to fill us with His Spirit. We also had prayer roads on the way to the airport and on the way to school.

Our son-in-law Jon recently told us that he and the children have also christened a stretch of highway on the way to school a "prayer road"—

just as they turn left onto Pineville Matthews Road. "Dear Jesus," one of the kids will pray from the back of the van. "We need Your love today. Help us to please You in everything we say, do, and think."

Having a prayer road is a wonderful metaphor for your relationship with God. It's an adventure, a journey, an experience you share together as you learn to trust and obey.

Getting to Know
Your New Friend

To Read to Your Children

When you meet new friends, how do you get to know them? The best way is to spend time with them. If a new friend wrote you a letter or sent you an e-mail, you would read it over and over and think about it, wouldn't you? When you invite Jesus to be your new friend, you'll want to learn all about Him. You'll want to have your very own Bible, a wonderful letter from God that will help you get to know who God is and what He likes.

The Bible explains everything about God and His Son, Jesus. It tells you that He created the world and lets you know why He made you and how much He loves you. The Bible teaches what is right and tells how to stay away from things that make God unhappy.

There are many books in the Bible—sixty-six of them! It's divided into two sections: the Old Testament and the New Testament. Some books tell you stories about people. There were many people who lived for God and did great things. But some people did not live to please God, and their stories are very sad. Other books are filled with poetry, songs, prayers, and instructions from God. Still others contain special messages from God to His people. The stories about Jesus, your new friend, begin in the New Testament.

Since you want to get to know God, you can study the Bible a little each day. You may choose to start by reading the Gospel of John.

Whenever you read a paragraph or verse in the Bible, it helps if you do two things: (1) ask God to help you understand His letter to you; and (2) stop and think about what you have just read.

Sometimes it helps to ask yourself two questions that begin with *What*: (1) "What does this say?" and (2) "What does it mean to me?" This is how you hear God's voice. It's good to think about the words a few minutes after you read them. You can ask God to speak to you in your heart through the words you have read.

The Bible teaches what is right and tells how to stay away from things that make God unhappy.

There are beautiful songs that keep God's words rolling over and over in your mind. These words will help you remember and want to do what God tells you to do. You'll like the song "Trust and Obey." It's fun to sing about being "happy in Jesus."

As you read your Bible and sing the songs you've learned, you will notice that you have a very happy feeling inside your heart. That's because you're spending time with your friend, the Lord Jesus. He knows how to make you happy. His Holy Spirit lives in your heart and will remind you that He loves you. He will give you ideas of things you can do that please God. He will help you to say "no" to things that are harmful and wrong, and "yes" to things that are good and right. You will enjoy a wonderful friendship and a great adventure as you learn to trust and obey God. That's something to smile about. What a great friend you have!

CHAPTER SEVEN
Welcome to the Family

Salvation Is Just the Beginning

The plane I (Robert) was riding was screaming into the sky directly south from the Nashville airport. I was headed to the West Coast, so as the plane banked sharply to the right, I got a glimpse of the area of the city where we lived, southwest of downtown.

Because it was early in the morning, the sunlight from the east was illuminating the tops of the huge oak trees below. It was an awesome panorama of our town. In a way that I had never seen before, the rays were also picking up every church steeple in Williamson County, punctuating them against the shadowed neighborhoods that surrounded them.

The man next to me leaned across to get a good look. "Wow, look at all those churches," he said. "They're everywhere."

We had lived in Nashville for more than a dozen years, but I had never noticed so many churches . . . many of them clumped together along the road—the prayer road—we traveled on our way to our own church.

Soon my plane punched through the low-lying cloud cover, obscuring the landscape below. I laid my head back and began to think about what I had just seen.[10] All of those churches down there gave me a sense of confidence. Of peace.

Even back when we both were kids, church played a vital role in our lives. It was a place where we were able to worship with a large group of Christians. It was a place where we met adults who believed what we believed—grown-ups who weren't teach-

> *All of those churches down there gave me a sense of confidence. Of peace.*

ers ("Finish your homework") or coaches ("Take another lap") or family ("I remember when you were just *this* tall"). They loved us enough to underscore what our parents were telling us about Jesus and of our need to trust and obey Him.

At church, we also met other Christ-following young people who provided a solid base of good friends. We simply could not have imagined life without our local church.

The Church on the Street Where You Live

Before churches had sanctuaries and pipe organs and steeples, they looked like homes. In fact, long before church buildings were ever constructed, churches *were* homes. Even today, many believers around the world meet in undercover house churches.[11] What they're doing is prohibited, but they're willing to risk their lives to meet together.

But in this context, we're not talking about house-churches like these where friends and neighbors gather. Whether you know it or not, your home is a "church". . . complete with its own "priest."

Back in the Old Testament, before official priests were selected to lead the Jews in worship, this assignment was given to fathers in their home. Noah and Job were examples of ordinary fathers who ushered their families into God's presence in repentance, in restoration, and in worship.[12]

And even though you and I have the responsibility—the privilege—of being involved with a local church congregation, our home is also a church . . . and we are the priests. "You are a chosen people, a royal priesthood, a holy nation, a people belonging to God" (1 Peter 2:9, NIV).

Before official priests were selected to lead the Jews in worship, this assignment was given to fathers in their home.

As the priests in our homes, our job description includes introducing our kids to the Savior and leading them in Bible reading, prayer, and singing. Our task is to guide our children as they walk with Jesus day after day. This is discipleship . . . *bringing* them along in the faith. (Whole Heart Ministries has developed an excellent resource to help families live out the values of a Christ-centered home. See "Our 24 Family Ways" on page 99.)

Your child will also need reassurance of his or her place in God's Kingdom. Even when the transaction between young people and their heavenly Father is completed, there will be times when they will wonder if they should go back and do it again. Your children need to hear that God will never let them go.

Here's what the apostle Paul said: "For I am sure that neither death nor life, nor angels nor rulers, nor things present nor things to come, nor powers, nor height nor depth, nor anything else in all creation, will be able to separate us from the love of God in Christ Jesus our Lord" (Romans 8:38-39, ESV).

These words assure you that your child's adoption into God's family creates an unbreakable bond. Of course, just as this is true with you, their lives will be a continual process of spiritual growth through the confession of their sin and a renewal of their desire to follow Christ.

Remember all those church steeples visible from the sky? If we could catch a glimpse of all the house-churches, there wouldn't be dozens of churches below; there would be hundreds upon hundreds of them. Maybe thousands of churches in our county alone.

The same is true in your town—and your home is one of them.

Your Home Church's Missions Program

The introduction to this book tells the story of how Bobbie met Jesus through a family—a neighborhood "house church"—across the street from her home. Without really thinking about it, this family, the Lays, had a missions program . . . their children were the missionaries and their neighborhood was the mission field.

Sharing the love of Jesus is one of the great joys of your Christ-following family. For many of the children who walk across the threshold of your house, this is the first and *only* Christian home they've ever encountered. As God's ambassador, your open arms and loving spirit will be the first time they meet Jesus.

On the playground, your children will have a chance to be miniature ministers. One of our friends, a young mother, told us that one afternoon her little girl encountered a bully in the sandbox at the city park.

TABLE TALK

So much of your "ministry" to your kids in your "house church" will be found in the ordinary moments . . . like conversation around the dinner table.

When our children were small, we tried to kick-start good conversation around the dinner table with two questions: "What was your happiest thing today?" and "What was your saddest thing today?" This always evoked interesting family talk. We thought it was a good way to get the kids involved in the discussion.

But when we met Henry—the author of many books, including *Experiencing God*—and Marilynn Blackaby, we learned a whole new way of focusing family talk.

Each evening as the family sat together around the dinner table, Henry and Marilynn would ask their kids, "What did God say to you today?" This is a *great* idea. Imagine how Richard, Tom, Mel, Norman, and Carrie would keep their eyes and ears tuned for God's activity in their life during the day, anticipating the time they could give a report to their family at dinner.[13]

From the moment the girl stepped into the sand, the mean boy taunted and teased her. Then he began throwing fistfuls of sand into her hair. Finally, after she had had enough of his rudeness, the girl headed for the jungle gym. As she was stepping out of the sandbox, she turned to her tormenter. "God loves you," she said.

Your children catch this "missionary" spirit from you as they watch the way you interact with your neighbors, speak to store clerks who wait on you, and treat service contractors who come to your home to repair things. Your kids observe you in these settings and will probably imitate how you care for others without even thinking about it.

As our friend's young daughter was stepping out of the sandbox, she turned to her tormenter. "God loves you," she said.

By the time they were twelve years old, our daughters were in considerable demand as babysitters. They took a backpack loaded with special things to their assignments, making sure their visit with the kids would be lots of fun. Christian storybooks and a Bible were often included to be read to the children at bedtime.

Recently we received the quarterly publication from Brentwood Academy, the Christian high school our children attended. This issue included the awards given to graduates. One of the awards is for spiritual leadership. This year's recipient was Brandon Albright.

When Brandon was a toddler, his parents asked our daughter Julie to babysit. At bedtime, Julie pulled the Bible out of her backpack and read to Brandon and his brother, Justin. The Albrights continued to call her back for more babysitting, and so Julie often read to the boys from her Bible at bedtime.

One morning at breakfast, Justin and Brandon told their parents that they really liked the story Julie had read them from the Bible the night before. "Where did she find a Bible in this house?" their mother asked. Although the family had had no particular interest in spiritual things before, Brandon and Justin's parents were fascinated with their sons' report.

Brandon's mother called us with questions, and soon their family was visiting our church. In time, Don and Julie Albright invited Jesus into their hearts and committed themselves to spiritual leadership in their family. The photo of their son in the school publication—now a handsome young Christian leader—is a reminder of God's grace and faithfulness, introduced by a little missionary many years before.

Your Church's Stewardship Campaign

Another way to help your children understand their call to be missionaries is to alert them to the need to give of their financial resources.

Many churches hold an annual fund-raising drive, usually in the fall. Of course, most of them are too diplomatic to call it what it is, so they refer to the program of encouraging their members to give money to the church a "stewardship campaign." But "stewardship" *is* really what the campaign is about.

As you might guess, the Bible says something about giving to the church: "Bring the whole tithe into the storehouse, that there may be food in my house. Test me in this," says the LORD Almighty, "and see if

I will not throw open the floodgates of heaven and pour out so much blessing that you will not have room enough for it" (Malachi 3:10, NIV).

Part of your priestly responsibility in your Christ-following home is to show your children how to give. Pressing a dollar into their little hands on their way to Sunday school begins to set a pattern. Once they are old enough to earn money for themselves, teach them the importance of setting some of it aside for God's work.

The principle here is not that we tip God like we would a skycap at the airport, then go our way. No, we are acknowledging who really owns it all. Giving a portion of our money back to God is a reminder to Him—and to us—that everything we have is on loan from Him. We are "stewards" or caretakers of His property. Our generosity is a reminder to us and to our children that, in the end, everything belongs to God.

The Prayers of the Priest

Prayer is something we have the privilege of doing for our own family "congregation." Nothing is more important. And if we need a place to start, the apostle Paul gives us words we can pray for each person in our families. "I do not cease to give thanks for you, remembering you in my prayers, that the God of our Lord Jesus Christ, the Father of glory, may give you a spirit of wisdom and of revelation in the knowledge of Him" (Ephesians 1:16-17, ESV).

Part of your priestly responsibility in your Christ-following home is to show your children how to give.

In many formal churches, the priest faces the altar with his back to the congregation as he prays for the people. This is a great picture of how we, like an attorney before the judge, can plead mercy for others before the heavenly throne.

The best prayers to pray for our children come directly from your Bible. We know a dad who writes in the margin of his Bible, next to portions of Scripture, the name of his child and the date he prayed that verse for his child.

Here are some great ones for you to use.

- "For this reason I bow my knees before the Father, from whom every family in heaven and on earth is named, that according to the riches of His glory He may grant you to be strengthened with power through His Spirit in your inner being, so that Christ may dwell in your hearts through faith." (Ephesians 3:14-17, ESV)
- "When I called, you answered me; You made me bold and stouthearted." (Psalm 138:3, NIV)
- "When He, the Spirit of truth, comes, He will guide you into all truth. He will not speak on His own; He will speak only what He hears, and He will tell you what is yet to come." (John 16:13, NIV)

A mother we know uses the direct approach when it comes to praying for her kids. Every morning before they leave for school, she asks, "How can I pray for you today?" One day her five-year-old son said, "I think you better pray for the mean boy in my class. Pray that he won't be bad today." The boy's mom had her assignment.

Praying for your children will become a lifelong adventure for you. A few months before he died, I (Robert) sat with my dad in my parents' home. Dad was suffering from a rare neurological disease that rendered him quiet and withdrawn. He had a hard time talking or listening. His eyes were failing so he couldn't read the newspaper or watch the news on television.

"Dad," I said to him, "how does all of this make you feel?"

He looked straight into my eyes. "Useless," he said.

"Dad," I finally said after a few minutes. "Do you remember how you used to pray for us?"

"I still do," Dad returned with a faint smile.

"Do you know what a difference that makes in our lives? Do you know how thankful we are?"

He nodded.

"Even if you were able-bodied and strong," I continued, "there still is nothing more important—more useful—that you could do than to keep praying."

"Do you know what a difference that makes in our lives? Do you know how thankful we are?"

"You're right . . . thank you, Son," Dad added.

"No, thank *you*," I said as I walked over to his chair. Kneeling down in front of my dad, I put my arms around him and hugged him.

"Thank you," I repeated, kissing him on the cheek. I held my father for just a few more moments and kissed him again.

One month later, Dad went Home.[14]

Follow, Then Lead

As a Christ-following parent, you must grow in your own love for Jesus Christ. Nurture that faith as you stand in the presence of a holy and awesome God and as you seek to know Him through prayer, Bible study, and fellowship with other believers.

And as you follow Him and pray for your family, God will give you everything you need to lead your child to the threshold of their own journey of faith.

As you therefore have received Christ Jesus the Lord, so walk in Him,
rooted and built up in Him and established in the faith, as you have been taught,
abounding in it with thanksgiving. (Colossians 2:6-7)

Growing in God's Garden

To Read to Your Children

Have you ever planted a seed and watched it turn into a big, green plant? It takes a lot of sunshine and water for the seed to grow. Pretty soon a tiny stem appears, and after a while green leaves pop out. The leaves point up toward the sun to grow even stronger. The roots grow down deeper and deeper to drink water. The next thing you know, you see a beautiful flower, a healthy vegetable, or a yummy fruit. If you've ever eaten a sweet grape or a crunchy apple, remember that it started as a tiny little seed.

When your friendship with Jesus grows, you're like that little seed. After you prayed and asked Jesus to forgive your sins, it was like you were planted in God's garden. Now, little by little, you will grow to be a strong follower of Jesus. This will happen as you read or listen to God's Word and learn to know Him better. You will grow as you go to church and Sunday school. That's where you learn about Jesus Christ and meet with other people who are following Him. You will grow when you give some of your money to your church. You will grow when you sing songs that keep thoughts about God in your mind. You will grow every time you pray and thank God for good food to eat. You will even grow at night when you say your prayers. Before you go to sleep is a great time to think about a Bible verse or the words to a hymn. And you can ask the Lord to be with you all night while you are sleeping.

One of the wonderful things God wants you to do after you become a Christian is to grow like a strong plant that produces good fruit. When you read the Bible, pray, go to church, give your money, and sing songs that fill your mind with the sunshine of God's love, good things will happen. The Bible says that love, joy, peace, patience, kindness, goodness, faithfulness, gentleness, and self-control are like fruit that grows if you love Jesus and let God's Spirit live in you (Galatians 5:22-23, NIV). When other people see you bursting with good fruit like this, they will know you have asked the Lord Jesus to help you grow in His garden.

And there's something else that happens when you grow. Every time you tell your friends about the love of Jesus, you will be planting seeds that may grow into new Christians. That's the most fun of all. If you see a friend or someone in your family with a little seed of faith, it will make you very happy to see that person grow to love Jesus more and more. You'll feel so happy that you will jump up and down. That's how God plans for His garden to grow. He is happy, too, when your family and friends grow into strong followers of His Son, Jesus.

Jesus wants you to grow close to Him. To make sure that happens, be sure to stay in the sunshine of God's love—read your Bible, pray every day, go to church, be generous with your money, sing songs of praise to God, and tell others about His wonderful love. The more you grow to be like God's Son, Jesus, the more great things you'll be able to do for God.

The Apostles' Creed

Being on God's Team—
To Read to Your Children

Have you ever been to a ball game and listened as everyone shouted for his or her team? The fans say special cheers together like "We've got spirit, yes we do, we've got spirit, how about you?" Everyone is encouraged to be winners when they cheer together.

Jesus and His followers are a team. The first Christians needed something like a cheer that they could say. It would help them remember that they were all on the same team. It would also help them remember what they believed. They called their cheer the Apostles' Creed. It was called a creed because the word *creed* means "I believe."

The twelve men who were Jesus' disciples are also called apostles. That means they were with Jesus while He lived on earth, and they followed Him. Even though you and I have not actually seen Jesus, we know that He is with us because He says in the Bible that He will always be with us. When we have asked Jesus to come and live in our hearts, we are like the apostles. We follow Jesus by obeying Him and following what He teaches us in the Bible. Because we follow Jesus, we can "listen" to His voice speaking in our heart.

During worship services, Christians all around the world say the Apostles' Creed together as a reminder of what all of us believe about God, about Jesus, and about the Holy Spirit. It makes us feel strong to be able to speak what we believe. Saying the Apostles' Creed also makes us feel close to Christians in other places. When we say it together, it's like giving a cheer for Jesus and the rest of our team.

The Apostles' Creed says what Christians believe about God, about Jesus, and about the Holy Spirit.

Listen to the Apostles' Creed and say it aloud until you have memorized it. If someone asks you, "What do you believe?" these words will help you to say exactly what that is.

✳ ✳ ✳

I believe in God, the Father Almighty, the Creator of heaven and earth.

And in Jesus Christ, His only Son, our Lord:

Who was conceived by the Holy Spirit, born of the virgin Mary,

Suffered under Pontius Pilate, was crucified, died, and was buried.

He descended into hell.

The third day He arose again from the dead.

He ascended into heaven and sits at the right hand of God the Father, Almighty.

From there He shall come to judge the living and the dead.

I believe in the Holy Spirit, the holy Christian church, the communion of saints,

The forgiveness of sins, the resurrection of the body,

And life everlasting. Amen.

The Lord's Prayer

The Best Call You Can Make—
To Read to Your Children

One of the best things about having God's Son, Jesus, as your friend is that you can tell Him everything, whether it's good or bad, and He will always listen to you. He loves you and always has time for you.

Talking with God through His Son is called prayer. You can pray anytime and anywhere, out loud or silently in your heart.

Jesus said that everyone who believes in Him is a child in God's family. There is one prayer that Jesus taught His friends to say. He wanted everyone in God's family to know how to get in touch with His heavenly Father anytime, day or night.

Do you remember when your dad or mom taught you your phone number? They told you to memorize it so you can call them whenever you need them or when you just want to talk to them.

One day Jesus' twelve disciples asked Him how they could call God, His Father in heaven. They wanted Him to teach them how to pray. Jesus told them they could repeat these words any time and in any place. Then God (their Father too) would listen. Do you know what the words are? They're in a special prayer called the Lord's Prayer. Some people call it the "Our Father." It is a prayer that God's children have prayed together for hundreds of years. You can memorize it and say it whenever you like. You can say it whenever you are together with your church family.

The Lord's Prayer is a way for you to keep in touch with your heavenly Father. Once you learn this prayer, you'll know what kinds of things you can talk to God about. You can use the words in the prayer Jesus taught. And you can pray about the same kinds of things in your own words, too.

Listen to the Lord's Prayer and pretty soon you will be praying right along. You will be calling your Father in heaven and talking to Him with the words that God's Son, Jesus, told His friends to pray.

You won't need a telephone for this conversation. Let's go ahead and call our heavenly Father right now!

❋ ❋ ❋

Our Father, who art in heaven,
Hallowed be Thy name.
Thy kingdom come, Thy will be done,
On earth as it is in heaven.
Give us this day our daily bread,
And forgive us our sins,
As we forgive those who sin against us.
And lead us not into temptation,
But deliver us from evil,
For Thine is the kingdom, and the power,
And the glory, forever. Amen.

Our 24 Family Ways

Some young parents introduced us to a wonderful program developed by Clay Clarkson, director of Whole Heart Ministries. It's called "Our 24 Family Ways" and is the foundation of a family discipleship tool called *Our 24 Family Ways: Family Devotional Guide* that includes 120 family devotionals, each based on one of the family "ways." (Whole Heart Ministries also developed the companion *Our 24 Family Ways Kids Color-In Book* for parents to use with young children.[15])

This powerful collection of character-building affirmations can provide a strong foundation of Christian habits in your home. Even though no family could be expected to instantly absorb all of these "ways," we found them to be a fantastic list of Christian family goals and priorities. You might want to soak in one "way" per month for twenty-four months, looking for opportunities to put them to use with your family. Imagine what your home would feel like after two short years of doing this!

Concerning AUTHORITIES in our family . . .

1. We love and obey our Lord, Jesus Christ, with wholehearted devotion.
2. We read the Bible and pray to God every day with an open heart.

3. We honor and obey our parents in the Lord with a respectful attitude.

4. We listen to correction and accept discipline with a submissive spirit.

Concerning RELATIONSHIPS in our family . . .

5. We love one another, treating others with kindness, gentleness, and respect.

6. We serve one another, humbly thinking of the needs of others first.

7. We encourage one another, using only words that build up and bless others.

8. We forgive one another, covering an offense with love when wronged or hurt.

Concerning POSSESSIONS in our family . . .

9. We are thankful to God for what we have, whether it is a little or a lot.

10. We are content with what we have, not coveting what others have.

11. We are generous with what we have, sharing freely with others.

12. We take care of what we have, using it wisely and responsibly.

Concerning WORK in our family . . .

13. We are diligent to complete a task promptly and thoroughly when asked.

14. We take initiative to do all of our own work without needing to be told.

15. We work with a cooperative spirit, freely giving and receiving help.

16. We take personal responsibility to keep our home neat and clean at all times.

Concerning ATTITUDES in our family . . .

17. We choose to be joyful, even when we feel like complaining.

18. We choose to be peacemakers, even when we feel like arguing.

19. We choose to be patient, even when we feel like getting our own way.

20. We choose to be gracious, even when we don't feel like it.

Concerning CHOICES in our family . . .

21. We do what we know is right, regardless of what others do or say.

22. We ask before we act when we do not know what is right to do.

23. We exercise self-control at all times and in every kind of situation.

24. We always tell the truth and do not practice deceitfulness of any kind.

CD Song Lyrics

Into My Heart
Harry D. Clarke

> Into my heart, into my heart,
> Come into my heart, Lord Jesus.
> Come in today, come in to stay,
> Come into my heart, Lord Jesus.

Holy, Holy, Holy!
Reginald Heber

1. Holy, holy, holy! Lord God Almighty!
   Early in the morning our song shall rise to Thee.
   Holy, holy, holy! Merciful and mighty!
   God in three Persons, blessed Trinity!

2. Holy, holy, holy! All the saints adore Thee,
   Casting down their golden crowns around the glassy sea;
   Cherubim and seraphim falling down before Thee,
   Who wert, and art, and evermore shall be.

3. Holy, holy, holy! Though the darkness hide Thee,
   Though the eye of sinful man Thy glory may not see,
   Only Thou art holy; there is none beside Thee
   Perfect in pow'r, in love, and purity.

4. Holy, holy, holy! Lord God Almighty!
   All Thy works shall praise Thy name in earth and sky and sea.

Holy, holy, holy! Merciful and mighty!
God in three Persons, blessed Trinity!

What Can Wash Away My Sin?
Robert Lowry

1. What can wash away my sin? Nothing but the blood of Jesus;
   What can make me whole again? Nothing but the blood of Jesus.
   O precious is the flow that makes me white as snow;
   No other fount I know, nothing but the blood of Jesus.

2. For my cleansing this I see—Nothing but the blood of Jesus;
   For my pardon this my plea—Nothing but the blood of Jesus.
   O precious is the flow that makes me white as snow;
   No other fount I know, nothing but the blood of Jesus.

3. Nothing can for sin atone—Nothing but the blood of Jesus;
   Naught for good that I have done—Nothing but the blood of Jesus.
   O precious is the flow that makes me white as snow;
   No other fount I know, nothing but the blood of Jesus.

4. This is all my hope and peace—Nothing but the blood of Jesus;
   This is all my righteousness—Nothing but the blood of Jesus.
   O precious is the flow that makes me white as snow;
   No other fount I know, nothing but the blood of Jesus.

5. Now by this I'll overcome—Nothing but the blood of Jesus;
   Now by this I'll reach my home—Nothing but the blood of Jesus.
   O precious is the flow that makes me white as snow;
   No other fount I know, nothing but the blood of Jesus.

I Have Decided to Follow Jesus
Composer unknown

1. I have decided to follow Jesus;
   I have decided to follow Jesus;

I have decided to follow Jesus;
No turning back, no turning back.

2. Though none go with me, still I will follow;
Though none go with me, still I will follow;
Though none go with me, still I will follow;
No turning back, no turning back.

3. The world behind me, the cross before me;
The world behind me, the cross before me;
The world behind me, the cross before me;
No turning back, no turning back.
No turning back, no turning back.

Trust and Obey
John Sammis

1. When we walk with the Lord in the light of His Word,
What a glory He sheds on our way!
While we do His good will, He abides with us still,
And with all who will trust and obey.
Trust and obey, for there's no other way
To be happy in Jesus, but to trust and obey.

2. Not a shadow can rise, not a cloud in the skies,
But His smile quickly drives it away;
Not a doubt or a fear, not a sigh nor a tear,
Can abide while we trust and obey.
Trust and obey, for there's no other way
To be happy in Jesus, but to trust and obey.

3. Not a burden we bear, not a sorrow we share,
But our toil He does richly repay;
Not a grief nor a loss, not a frown or a cross,
But is blessed if we trust and obey.

Trust and obey, for there's no other way
To be happy in Jesus, but to trust and obey.

4. But we never can prove the delights of His love
   Until all on the altar we lay;
   For the favor He shows, and the joy He bestows,
   Are for those who will trust and obey.
   Trust and obey, for there's no other way
   To be happy in Jesus, but to trust and obey.

5. Then in fellowship sweet we will sit at His feet,
   Or we'll walk by His side in the way;
   What He says we will do, where He sends we will go—
   Never fear, only trust and obey.
   Trust and obey, for there's no other way
   To be happy in Jesus, but to trust and obey.

Endnotes

1. *Adapted from* Passion Hymns for a Kid's Heart *by Bobbie Wolgemuth and Joni Eareckson Tada (Wheaton, Ill.: Crossway Books, 2005) and used with permission of the publisher.*

2. *King David's only instruction was for us to make a joyful noise (see Psalm 96).*

3. *Blaise Pascal (1623–1662), a French-born child prodigy, mathematician, and inventor; converted to Christianity at age thirty-one.*

4. *See John 3:3.*

5. *Your favorite Christian bookstore is stocked with toddler Bibles with plastic handles, such as* My First Bible in Pictures *by Kenneth Taylor (Wheaton: Tyndale, 1989).*

6. *Adapted from* She Calls Me Daddy *by Robert Wolgemuth (Wheaton: Tyndale, 1996), 147–149.*

7. *Dr. Chuck Swindoll has said that if Jesus hadn't called Lazarus by name, everybody in the entire graveyard would have obeyed His directive and stepped out into the sunlight!*

8. *John Sammis, "Trust and Obey," 1887.*

9. *Adapted from* The Most Important Place on Earth *by Robert Wolgemuth (Nashville: Thomas Nelson, 2004), 31–32.*

10. *Story excerpted from* The Most Important Place on Earth *by Robert Wolgemuth (Nashville: Thomas Nelson, 2004), 201–202.*

11. *In China alone, there are hundreds of thousands of house churches.*

12. *This idea of parents as priests is more full developed in chapter 10 of* The Most Important Place on Earth.

13. *The Blackaby's sons each have their doctorates in various biblical disciplines and their daughter, Carrie, has her master's degree in Christian education and is, with her husband, Wendell, a career missionary in Germany. As grownups, God is still speaking to them.*

14. *Adapted from* Prayers from a Dad's Heart *by Robert Wolgemuth (Grand Rapids: Inspirio, the gift group of Zondervan, 2003). Used with permission from the publisher.*

15. *The following list is reprinted with permission of Clay Clarkson and Whole Heart Ministries, copyright ©1998. For more information, see http://www.wholeheart.org.*

FOCUS ON your child®
FROM FOCUS ON THE FAMILY®

enjoy the journey™

Does parenting sometimes seem like an overwhelming task? Your role as a parent is difficult but very important to you and your children, and Focus on the Family® wants to encourage you! The complimentary Focus on Your Child® membership program has age-specific materials that provide timely encouragement, advice and information for today's busy parents. With newsletters or audio journals delivered straight to your doorstep once a month and a Web site packed with over 900 articles, Focus on Your Child can help you enjoy the journey!

Here's what the membership includes:

Parenting Newsletters: Four age-specific and concise editions for parents with no spare time.

Audio Journals: Timely information for parents and fun activities for children, based on their ages.

Online Resources: Age-customized articles, e-mail news, recommended resources and topic-organized forum through which parents can share with one another.

To sign up, go to www.focusonyourchild.com or call (800) A-FAMILY.

YF05XPRD